Writers of Wales

EDITORS

MEIC STEPHENS   R. BRINLEY JONES

D. J. WILLIAMS

1885-1970

Dafydd Jenkins

D. J. WILLIAMS

*University of Wales Press
on behalf of the Welsh Arts Council*

1973

w 891.66 J/L = 8WIL (048)
32
JEN

891.66 32WIL
JEN

35761

'

a 0708304615

13/3/91

I

Mr Saunders Lewis—now, in his seventies, both *doyen* and *enfant terrible* of Welsh literary criticism—has written several times about the work of his old associate in politics and crime, D. J. Williams, and has done so with such a mixture of perception and wrongheadedness that there is a great temptation to cast this essay into the form of a commentary on Mr Lewis's comments. I have resisted the temptation, though it will be clear to many readers that some of my observations have been provoked by those comments; indeed, I may well owe to their stimulus far more than I realise. I shall refer specifically to one or two of Mr Lewis's heresies in due course, and I shall take one of his comments as a general text.

Mr Lewis has doubted whether there is value in an evaluation in English of D. J. Williams's stature and importance as a writer. To him, the English translation of HEN DŷFFARM is a disaster, and the book is untranslatable. If either proposition is true—and I am not concerned to argue the point—that is the more reason for making the desperate effort to convey to the English reader something of the delight which we find in that untranslatable original. Men learn Greek in order to read the authentic Homer; to be able to read D. J. Williams is one of the richer rewards of mastering Welsh.

In spite of his doubts Mr Lewis went forward to

express an opinion: it was the *unique medley of literary Welsh and old, rich, traditional Carmarthenshire dialect*

that made D. J. Williams *a writer of importance and for the future a classic of a kind.*

Mr Lewis cannot have meant to imply that D.J.'s literary beauty was skin-deep. He would surely accept the principle stated by an earlier Welsh critic, Emrys ap Iwan:

Appropriate language is not a garment loosely hanging on the thought, but a body jointly begotten with it—a spiritual, transparent, body which serves only to give form to the man within, and not to hide him either.

D.J. wrote as he did because he thought and lived as he did. His writing could never have come from a 'creative artist' of the Art-for-Art's-sake school; its artistry is the glorious by-product of the integrity of a craftsman. D.J. was concerned to present as perfectly as he could the vision which he had received—a simple vision, and on a superficial view even a naïve one; but he received that vision precisely because of his integrity, and it was that same integrity which made of him a craftsman who could present the vision.

2

II

Born at another time and in another place, D. J. Williams must surely have written memorable prose on some subject in some language. But the fact that he wrote on the particular subjects which he chose in the particular language which he chose was determined by the accident of his birth—so that indeed it might be said that it was the subjects and the language which chose him, rather than he who chose them; and any study of his work must begin with an account of his life.

In his last years of literary activity D.J. wrote two volumes of autobiography without carrying the story beyond the age of 26, but the outward facts of his whole life can easily be compressed into a paragraph. He was born at Penrhiw Fawr in the parish of Llansawel in northern Carmarthenshire on 26 June 1885, and moved with his parents and sister to Abernant (a smaller farm a couple of miles away) in 1891. He left Abernant at the age of sixteen, to work underground in the Rhondda, at Betws near Ammanford, and at Seven Sisters in the Dulais Valley, for a total of five years. At 21 he resumed formal education, attending private schools which specialised in training grown men, taking correspondence courses, and working as an uncertificated teacher in Merioneth, until in 1911 he entered the University College of Wales, Aberystwyth. He went on to Oxford, taught for a year at Lewis's School, Pengam (where he was nicknamed 'Sunny Jim'), and for 26 years (with a break of a year) at Fishguard County School, and retired from teaching in 1945. He died, in the chapel at Rhydcymerau which he had attended as a boy, on 4 January 1970.

His literary biography can be set out with similar conciseness. He was a prolific writer on a variety of subjects from his student days at Aberystwyth, but the first of the works by which he must be judged appeared when he was already in his forties. This was one of a series of sketches of the characters of his native district which were to be collected into a volume, HEN WYNEBAU*, in 1934. By that date he had already turned to the short story, and in 1936 he published in STORÏAU'R TIR GLAS eight short stories; these included two sets of three stories each, which had won prizes

---

*The titles of D.J.'s books will be left untranslated, for a reason which will be quite clear when their meaning has been explained. HEN WYNEBAU is literally 'Old Faces', and might pass in English under that name; the titles of the volumes of stories cannot be put into English without losing the parallelism of the Welsh. 'Stories of the Land' renders STORÏAU'R TIR correctly enough, but the colours —green, red, and black—of the separate volumes cannot be applied to the word *land*. *Tir glas* means pasture; 'ploughland' would do for *tir coch;* but *tir du* must become 'black earth': it refers to peaty moorland soil, and the expression was specially chosen by D.J. as appropriate to the spiritual background of the stories. THE OLD FARM-HOUSE, the title of the English translation of HEN DŶ FFARM, has the definite article where literal correctness requires the indefinite; YN CHWECH AR HUGAIN OED means 'At Twenty-six Years of Age'.

The titles of sketches and stories will be translated or explained as seems most appropriate or convenient.

4

at the National Eisteddfod. This volume was followed by Storïau'r Tir Coch in 1941 and Storïau'r Tir Du in 1949, several of the stories in each having previously appeared in periodicals. The volumes of autobiography, Hen Dŷ Ffarm (1953) and Yn Chwech ar Hugain Oed (1959) were his last literary works, but in 1966 the selection Storïau'r Tir showed which of his stories he regarded as worth reprinting.

These paragraphs of biography give no real information about D. J. Williams. They are concerned with purely objective, essentially superficial, facts, and tell us nothing about the real man. He might himself have said that the first biographical sentence gave all the significant information about him, and that everything else in his life was only a working out of what was effectively determined by the place and time of his birth. To this the answer may well be the same as the answer to Johnson's assertion that once Swift had thought of big men and little men it was easy enough to write Gulliver's Travels, namely that the working out of even the most obvious design can require much effort. And our effort to understand the working out of D.J.'s destiny will be much helped if we take as starting point that parenthesis in his teaching career, the interval in 1936-37 when he was suspended from his post at Fishguard.

For the first months of his suspension he was awaiting trial, for most of the time he was serving a sentence of imprisonment, for his part in burning certain buildings on a site which was being developed as an R.A.F. bombing school, near Pwllheli in the Llŷn peninsula of Caernarvonshire. His companions in crime and punishment were Saunders Lewis and Lewis Valentine, who had been for some ten years his associates in the young Welsh Nationalist Party, not yet known as Plaid Cymru. The Party had conducted a public campaign of protest against the establishment of the bombing school; direct action was taken privately by the inner circle of the Party's leaders. Saunders Lewis was President and Valentine Vice-President of the Party; they became incendiaries *ex officio,* as it were. D. J. Williams was a founder member of the Party and served on its Executive Committee, but he held no special office: he was chosen from among the volunteers for a place behind the flames because of the affection which every member of the Party had for him, and because of the respect which his integrity and courage had won from his acquaintances outside the Party, even when they detested his politics.

To try to explain that affection is to run the risk of a charge of sentimentality or even blasphemy, but the risk must be taken, and those who felt that D.J. was their friend will not think it improper to say that we loved him because he first loved us. There was a radiance about him which made him more than approachable: rather, the approach came from him, he was always eager to know the latest, youngest, addition to the household of the faith. To the very end of his life he was happy—surely, at his happiest—in the company of the young men and women of the various branches of the nationalist movement.

6

This was no accident, it was the natural result of the particular character of his nationalism. In Wales as in other countries, some nationalists would say of their convictions that they bought their freedom with a great price; D. J. Williams was born free. So he claimed, less with pride than with acceptance of a natural, inevitable fact: to him the nationhood, the distinctiveness, of Wales was the vivifying element in the blessed society of his boyhood. The radiance of his personality reflected his vision of that society, it was dulled when he feared that society was doomed, and it was renewed in the company of those whom he saw coming forward to carry on his own struggle to save it.

Sir Owen Edwards was one of D.J.'s heroes, and it was said of him that his native Llanuwchllyn was the most important sight that he ever saw, and that for him Wales was Llanuwchllyn repeated and enlarged. The same sort of assertion could be made about D.J., and all his actions and writings fall into the pattern of a natural working out of the principle which that implies. It is usual to sum up his literary achievement by calling him the interpreter of his private 'Square Mile'; the expression was his own, but it was used by him to define the limits of the area surrounding his home at Abernant:

Though I could at that time give pretty accurate statistics for all the district's resources in dogs and cats, horses and cattle, turkeys, fowls, and geese—and sheep for that matter, though I was never much of an authority on them—from Cilwennau to Cae Melwas, and from Maes Teile to Llety Llwyn Chwith, yet I must admit that the perfect field of my knowledge was from the Hafodwen turn to the top of the hill above the Cart—'Cart and Horses by John Jenkins', according to the sign (licensed to sell Beer, Wines and Spirits)—and from the bank above Cwmcoedifor to the bank above Llywele, about a square mile of land . . .

There were some seven homes in this Square Mile: Llether Bledrig, Abernant, Cwmdu, Cwmcoedifor, Pant yr Onnen, Esgertylcau, and Hafodwen. The area which D.J. called *Yr Hen Ardal,* 'the Old District', was wider:

from Bwlch Cae Melwas to Bwlch Cefen Sarth and from Craig Dwrch to Darren Fowr

—but we need not be pedantic about using the names with exact correctness: either will do as a label for D.J.'s 'only spiritual home', love for which was 'the kernel of his patriotism'.

The society of the Square Mile or the Old District is the direct subject of most of D.J.'s important writing, but he has done much more than paint a nostalgic picture of a boyhood paradise. The society of that paradise as he remembered it (or as he idealised it—it matters not) was the standard by which every other phenomenon was measured.

It is impossible to express in a paragraph or two what that society meant to D. J. Williams: it meant everything that he put into his writings. And it is particularly hard to convey the right impression in English because there are no satisfactory English equivalents for the Welsh words which we would use without thinking.

8

The English word *nationalism,* to begin with, carries an aura which its Welsh counterpart lacks, and it is even more important that it lacks the aura of the Welsh word. *Nationalism* is so often a term of abuse in English because *nation* is confused with *state; cenedlaetholdeb* is a term of abuse only when used with all the false overtones of *nationalism,* and *cenedligrwydd* (too often used to translate *nationality* in the sense of state-citizenship) properly means national character or national identity. Moreover, the Welsh word *cenedl* (today meaning *nation*) was the medieval word for kindred or family, in the wider sense of the anthropologists' 'extended family'. For D.J. the Welsh nation was a family—an extended family whose nuclear family was the society of the Square Mile. And when he made much of newcomers to the household of the faith (the Welsh version of the text has the modern word for *family* where the English has *household*), he was welcoming those who had found the true home of the family.

The character of the society of the Square Mile can be summed up in the Welsh adjective *gwâr*: but how can that adjective be translated? The derivative *gwareiddiad* is usually translated accurately enough by *civilisation,* but the basic adjective applies to the naturally civilised person who needs no civilising. D. J. would surely have approved the argument that whereas the English usage suggests that man is rough and uncouth until polished by urban (or political) influences, the Welsh recognises a contrary truth, that a simple rural society can be naturally *gwâr*. The Danish girl in John Buchan's THE ISLAND OF

9

SHEEP coined by back-formation the word *couth:* let us say that the society of the Square Mile was couth.

That is, it was a society in which men did not readily hurt each other, but lived together reasonably peaceably. No doubt there were quarrels, between individuals and between families, but as D.J. depicts them the quarrels seldom or never grew into long-standing feuds—partly no doubt, because the parties knew they would have to live together and to depend much on each other; partly, too, because they did not take themselves too seriously. It might be more accurate to say that they did not take themselves too solemnly: D.J. himself was serious enough, but never solemn. And of course all this is not much more than a description of a family— or at least of a family which has not been bedevilled by the Victorian misapplication of Roman authoritarianism in a nominally Christian context. It can hardly be an accident that (if the Irish scholars are right) the original application of the word *gwâr* was to the son who fulfilled the duty of caring for his aged parents.

Speaking of his schooldays, D.J. said that in later life he had been able

to enjoy society of many kinds contentedly enough—on the farm, in the coal-mine, in college and school and prison and hospital. But I might as well express my feeling here, that the society most blessed in its equality of which I was ever a member was the society in the district of my boyhood where everyone knew each other and knew everything worth knowing about each other, through the generations; with the minister and

10

the schoolmaster (people from outside us, as it happened) as masters over us and servants to us at the same time, and the home and the chapel and the school, in that order, as the three safe pillars supporting our life.

At first sight, the mention of the school in this context is surprising, but the sentence just quoted introduces an account of the local schoolmasters of D.J.'s boyhood which makes his tribute to them wholly consistent with his usual condemnation of the educational system in Wales as an 'English murder machine' destroying the consciousness of national identity.

D. J. Williams did not trot out conventional critical clichés about the school, and he did not trot out conventional laudatory clichés about the chapel. In fact he was at some pains to correct the picture of Puritan respectability which the mid-twentieth-century Welsh town mind automatically conjures up from the word *chapel*: the 'Cart and Horses' at Rhydcymerau raised a son for the Calvinistic Methodist ministry, and the elders of the chapel refused as one man to bow the knee to the Baal of the presbytery in the matter of the pledge of total abstinence. It becomes quite clear from D.J.'s account that at Rhydcymerau at the end of the nineteenth century the chapel's significance was social. The district could show the outside world few striking achievements in culture or religion: for that community in that generation culture was not a matter of self-expression nor religion a matter of individual salvation. The secular culture represented by choir and Eisteddfod, and the religious practice represented by Sunday and weekday meetings, were alike essentially social phenomena.

Perhaps this means that the chapel was not really a centre of religious practice at all, though it was certainly at times the scene of intense (if often scholastic) theological argument. But if the society was not religious, it was essentially Christian. D.J. never really understood Mr Saunders Lewis's assertion that religion has nothing to do with morality; he might have been able to understand the doctrine of religionless Christianity, the truth that Christianity is not so much a religion as a way of life, for that was the fact behind the religious façade in the Old District. It is common form today to speak of Wales (and Britain and the world) as becoming increasingly pagan—a stupid slander on paganism, justified only by the baseless supposition that every belief which is not formally Christian is equally anti-Christian. Paganism is pre-Christian and may be on the road to Christianity; the civilised and urbanised deviations of today are post-Christian. Some of them are Pelagian, but most are not even as creditable as that, since they deny what Pelagianism asserts, that objective truths and values exist. And the real pagan knows—does not merely believe, but knows— that objective truths and values exist, for the real pagan is a countryman who has learnt from experience that the earth is very honest.

In the extended family society of D. J. Williams's boyhood the pagan virtue of honesty was more important than any formal profession of religious faith. That is why D.J. found it embarrassing that Dafydd 'r Efailfach should at the end of his life

12

have given in to the conventions, and why he wrote of the angels

I believe that there was more perplexity than true joy in their presence that evening when this witty and happy sinner, with the hoary head of his eighty years, was seen abandoning the field and asking for chapel membership.

And that too is why it was quite natural for D.J. to adapt scriptural quotations to very unscriptural contexts: he was sure enough of his faith not to have to be solemn about it.

If the family of the Square Mile, and the extended family of Wales, ever existed in their full glory outside D.J.'s vision of them, the glory had certainly departed by the mid-1930's. The Forestry Commission had taken over many of the farms from which D.J.'s contemporaries had come to school, and in the mining valleys which had been so prosperous and lively when he worked there at the beginning of the century long-continued depression had driven away to new industries in England the liveliest of the young workers, leaving the others behind to break their hearts in an idleness which rotted into unemployability. The realisation that the 'gentlemen sitting in London' who governed the United Kingdom, and those others who ran its industry, recognised no responsibility towards Wales as a nation had made D.J. an active political nationalist long before 1936, and he had by that time been writing political articles for some twenty years; but it was then that his creative writing began to show a change of attitude. It

can hardly be a mere coincidence that the first
of his short stories to delve into the psychology
of a complex central character was written
during the period around the burning of the
bombing school. He did not at once forsake his
old subjects, and he never really changed his
style, but in 1936 he was coming to the end of his
first period.

Though there is some overlapping between the
periods—and especially between the first and
second—they are distinctive enough. The first
period is that of the sketches of HEN WYNEBAU,
most of the stories of the TIR GLAS, and some of
those of the TIR COCH, which present the old
society of the Square Mile. The sketches are
stills which sometimes have the careful detail of
a Breughel painting; the short stories catch some
corner of the scene in significant motion; but
every sketch or story is not only a complete
work in itself, it is also a living element in the
portrait of the whole society.

During that first period D. J. Williams had
perfected his technique as a story writer handling
simple themes. In the second period he was
concerned to move forward by using that
technique to grapple with deeper problems,
presented through more complex characters. He
had begun by re-creating, almost subconsciously,
the characters and events suggested to him by his
memory of that well-loved community, but he
went on to probe beneath the subsiding surface
of contemporary Wales in search of the under-
mining weaknesses. His themes now seem more
deliberately chosen for study: he takes a super-

14

ficially commonplace situation and makes a conscious effort to understand how the situation came about.

In this second period, already beginning in STORÏAU'R TIR GLAS, carrying on through most of the stories of STORÏAU'R TIR COCH, and culminating in STORÏAU'R TIR DU, his work was less obviously successful and certainly less attractive to the critics, and it was partly a feeling that the labour involved in cultivating the black earth was inadequately rewarded that led him to abandon the short story. In the two volumes of autobiography which mark the third period, D.J. returned first to the society of his boyhood and youth, depicting it now on a larger scale and in greater detail. Then, going on to tell of his working years in the South Wales coalfield and in preparation for entry to the University, he presented a different society in which significant changes were already obvious; and the indications of those changes become the occasion for a clear expression of that criticism of mid-twentieth-century Wales which is implied in one way or another in all the later short stories.

III

The masterpiece of the first period is HEN WYNEBAU—considered as a single composition, for though nine of the ten chapters appeared separately over a period of six years, they were deliberately rearranged so that they form a co-ordinated whole. The title suggests a gallery of individual portraits, but the book is in fact a single cunningly-drawn portrait of the society of the Square Mile, though the elements of this larger portrait are themselves portraits, on varying scales, of individual members of the society, with a single chapter which establishes a sort of frame of reference for the society in terms of family relationships.

To change the metaphor from the art gallery to the stage, HEN WYNEBAU is not a series of unconnected one-act plays but a sort of revue with a single theme. The performance begins with a prologue 'Dafydd 'r Efailfach', whose first sentence presents obliquely the deceptive theme:

Dafydd 'r Efailfach was the only man in the Old District who was out of the ordinary.

The district, we are to believe, was entirely ordinary: it was a comfortable society without great leaders or distinguished public figures, a part of the country of which no one had ever heard—happy, perhaps, because it had no history. But the next sentences give the game away:

But his gift was so peculiarly natural and effortless that many of the locals, I believe, could not see much difference between him and any other man. . . . However, my opinion of Dafydd is—that never man spake like this man, outside Synge's plays. But it would take another Synge to prove it in black and white.

In the original Welsh, those sentences show that Dafydd 'r Efailfach came close enough to finding his Synge, for if, as D.J. put it

Dafydd was Puck, forced to dress in Bottom's homespun,

D.J. himself was Puck imperfectly disguised in an usher's gown.

The lesson of Dafydd's prologue is that Puck can see every ordinary man as extraordinary, and that lesson will be underlined in all the scenes which follow, as D. J. Williams brings his characters onto the stage to show that the mildest of them can strut and fret to some purpose for at least a moment or two.

The scene which follows the prologue introduces nearly all the company, though they appear in groups and very few of them have speaking parts. The title of this scene is 'Y Tri Llwyth'—the Three Tribes—and for once the biblical word is used with complete accuracy, since the members of each tribe were descendants of a common ancestor. But the common ancestors were not contemporaries like the sons of Jacob: they were leaders of successive waves which D.J. compares with the Iberians, the Celts, and the Saxons. He himself was one of the aboriginal Iberians, the

Llywele tribe, and was proud to record that his grandfather was of the sixteenth generation to be born at Llywele. But it was the destiny of this tribe to be

almost squeezed out of the district, and there are some of the tribe in the five continents,

and he was

far away from my old dear countryside, earning my keep in a doubtful manner, while my untidy slug-ridden garden daily casts in my teeth my fall from the honourable lineage of mattock and spade.

For that matter, Llywele was well fitted to be the last refuge of a hunted people:

This pleasant old farmhouse stands in the middle of a fine level upland, which forms a sort of natural platform above the whole of the north of the county. The lark's industrious song in the heights, the sheep's bleat, and the distant whisper of the little stream alone break the silence. From its top can be seen a great part of Carmarthenshire, as well as a pretty clear glimpse of the far-off peaks of Pembrokeshire, Glamorgan, and Breconshire. The long ridge of the mountain range which runs from Pumlumon to the Frenni Fawr separates it from Cardiganshire, whose boundary is some six or seven miles away. The man who first chose this place for human habitation had an eye for security, for a livelihood, and for a glorious breadth of view. On three sides of it are the narrow deep rifts of Cwm Gorlech, Cwm Acheth, and Cwm Du. Someone compared Llywele to heaven—one of the pilgrims to Llangeitho long ago, like enough, after climbing the steep paths to it—as a place which was very hard to get to, but when reached a pleasant and delectable spot.

18

The Celts of the Old District were *Tylwyth y Doleydd*—the family of the three Dolau farms, Upper, Middle, and Lower. It was an old-established tribe in the male line,

but as it were yesterday or the day before as time is measured in an old district—or about a hundred years ago as it is measured by empires—romance brought a young woman called Anna into the family, from somewhere near Llandysul beyond the Teifi,

and her sons occupied the three farms in D.J.'s boyhood. The chieftain of the tribe was

a man of such size and fearsome aspect that his like was hardly to be found in the land. A leonine red head; freckled paws; and fingers and thumbs like the beams of an old house. No policeman was needed when he was around . . . A single roar from him would cause terror through a whole crowd . . . And yet, as his title shows—he was 'Uncle Tom' to all the district—he was beloved of everybody.

The Cnwc Tribe,

descendants of a young couple from Cardiganshire who began their married life in a farm of that name

just before 1850, were the

people who always stay behind to carry on the work when society is breaking up—when the imagination of the 'Iberian' sinks into barren hopelessness and the artistry of the 'Celt' is no more than the plaything of an idle hour.

In practical terms they were honest workers who had made their way because they could be relied on. But the reader can guess that no single individual stood out among them, for though D. J. Williams says nothing of this, he mentions no one by name as he picked out the Dolau brothers. Rather he makes the lack of outstanding features in the Cnwc tribe the great characteristic of the whole district—a peaceful neighbourly countryside just because no one had the ambition to be seen of men. The only disadvantage of this lack of 'leading horses' was that it tended to make progress in the harmless necessary committees (there were few enough of them) rather slow.

The rest of the revue is made up of solos and duets, ending with an epilogue. In sober literary terms, there are eight chapters, each dealing with one particular character, save that one chapter has twin characters as its subject. Three of the characters are animals: a sheepdog, a greyhound, and an old nag. The old nag has a solo to himself, and a walking-on part in the item devoted to his owner; the greyhound shares with his owner-twin the most satisfying in its rounded perfection of all D. J. Williams's sketches:

If you had met Ben Ty'n Grug and his greyhound on the road you would have sworn they were twins; and you would not have been very far out. In the long course of their development one could imagine that the souls of the two had at some time met in the same mould, and that they had ever afterwards tried to keep as close together as circumstances would allow. Or indeed, who knows that they were not a reincarnation of that strange greyhound of Deio Cwmgarw's long ago, which split in two from nose to tail when two hares started up before it at the same time—and caught them both, too? . . .

At any rate, the most perfect harmony and understanding flourished between Ben and his greyhound. On a cold or wet morning, if a shivering drop hung from Ben's nose, there would be a solemn drop of sympathy on Llwyd the grey-hound's nose, and on a hot summer day they would swelter wearily together as they longed for the same shade. . . .

The epilogue is one of the three long chapters; it forms an epilogue because in it D.J. looks back at the Old District from outside, through an outsider, 'Dafydd Ifans y Siop':

Dafydd Ifans the Shop lived in the Old District for nearly sixty years without a break; and he was an 'incomer' to the end. That's incredible, you say. It is, except to the locals. And I'm almost certain that none of them realised the fact, though they knew it well in the depth of their hearts.

But like the schoolmaster and the minister, this shopkeeper fulfilled a function which the locals themselves could not fulfil; and by simply standing out from the rest he serves in D.J.'s picture the purpose of emphasising the ordinari-ness of the Old District.

To put his point over, D.J. goes in for something of a *tour de force*. In the world of nations, he says,

the Englishman is more loud-mouthed and swaggering on the stations of the Continent because of the number of the chimneys of his enormous London; the Frenchman more mincing in his manner than any other man because his Paris is so elegant; and in every part of the world the Yankee's nasal drawl makes a heavy accompaniment to his tinkling dollar.
    But as for us in the Old District we had neither chimneys

nor dollars nor anything to draw attention to us. Ours was a commonplace district in everything, in the opinion of the surrounding districts; in land, in livestock, and in men— in exactly that order of importance. Llansawel had two whole streets of houses, three denominations, and six inns to boast of, as well as Rhydodyn mansion near by . . . At Talley, again, there was the old Abbey with its two bright lakes; while the praise of Abergorlech was sung over every hill and dale in the north of the county by Price of Bryn Cothi's hounds. . . . The only thing we had every day of the year was the Brynau bog in the middle and the steep slopes around it—and a noisier eisteddfod than the rest on Christmas Day. We could take pride too, especially at one period, in surprisingly good congregational singing. We tried to make up for every other defect by blind loyalty to the Old District on every occasion. But no—Dafydd Ifans the Shop lived in our district: a man whom no one could fail to respect, wherever he might be.

To the people of the Old District, the Shop family had

a certain air of distinction which subtly, very subtly, separated them from the rest of us;

D.J. suggests that this air sprang from the family's having come from a district where they might indirectly touch the hem of the county gentry's garment, while many of the people of Rhyd-cymerau were small freeholders who were

perhaps a little careless about the world's opinion and about due respect to our betters.

But perhaps it was the outward man in Dafydd Ifans that was most calculated to inspire respect; he was *a big, handsome man, fully six feet, with broad shoulders, robust, lively limbs, and a beard like a shield on his breast.*

And what if you saw him walking! The bend of the knee, the thrust of the foot, and the set of every limb, were in perfect harmony. The fine shapeliness of his body remained unimpaired until his last days, well beyond his eightieth birthday. He walked in a leisurely way, with a kind of modest dignity in his form and feature—as though one of the old Greek sages had returned to take the measure of the earth again. When I read as a boy of Caractacus in Rome, it was of Dafydd Ifans walking from the shop to the mill that I always thought.

For Dafydd Ifans's achievements in the Old District were modest—modest in sum and modest in manner. Much of the credit for that good congregational singing belonged to him: he brought to

a district which happened to be naturally rich in voices, with an ear for correctness of sound,

the enthusiasm for music which such men as Ieuan Gwyllt had aroused in many parts of Wales in the 1860's. But he never went in for competition much:

he had not enough self-confidence for that kind of thing. What he wanted was good singing, not victory in competition.

All this amounts to saying that he was a man very well suited to the district—different enough to make his neighbours conscious of his presence, similar enough for the presence not to irritate. In reforming mood he would expound his ideas to the children and urge them to proselytise their parents; but *as a rule his reforming zeal began and ended there. After all, there has to be a good deal of the bully in every successful reformer.*

And if D.J. pretended to take pride in the glory reflected on the Old District from the distinction of Dafydd Ifans, it's certain that he really took pride in the District's being so outwardly undistinguished.

IV

When D. J. Williams turned from the character sketches of HEN WYNEBAU to the short story, he did so (as we can see when we look back) because the short story would enable him to draw a truer picture on a broader canvas. In HEN WYNEBAU he had lovingly depicted an old remembered community, but it was a static community captured at a particular—perhaps an imaginary—moment of time. And there would be other experiences than those of the paradisal Rhydcymerau to record: the vision of Wales included scenes from the wilderness of this world also.

The earliest stories, nevertheless, show no sharp break with the world of HEN WYNEBAU: they tell of imaginary incidents, perhaps, but they are incidents which could have happened in that same world. Indeed, they may depict that world all the more truly because an imaginary incident must, if it is to be convincing, be more probable than a true one. Truth can be stranger than fiction, just because no one would believe it if it were fiction. And in turning to the short story D.J. was following an old tradition: for him, the short story was not a new literary form introduced into Wales by admirers of Chekhov and Maupassant. The ultimate ancestor of D. J. Williams is the medieval Welsh storyteller, the *cyfarwydd*.

Of course the typical medieval story is not a short story in the modern sense of the word: there always seems to be something disingenuous (or perhaps over-ingenuous?) about the popular collections of Short Stories of the World which include specimens from ancient Indian literature or traditional Celtic tales. But medieval Wales was precocious: the Red Book of Hergest (copied in the late fourteenth century from an older manuscript) contains one work which is not a mere romantic tale. 'The Dream of Rhonabwy' is a sophisticated, ironic, anti-romantic short story in the true sense of that technical expression, as a moment's comparison with the romance 'The Dream of Maxen Wledig', from the same source, will show. It would be easy enough to criticise the technique of 'The Dream of Rhonabwy': the author had not learnt to pitch his audience in at the deep end (though that indeed may be because he was composing a story to be read aloud in public) and his ending lacks crispness; but once he has set the scene, in his rather pedestrian way, at a particular time in a particular Welsh kingdom, his choice of events and of words to describe them creates a sharply-etched picture of contrast between the glorious Arthurian host of Rhonabwy's dream and (in Arthur's words)

such men of dirt as this, guarding this island after such good men as guarded it of old.

In medieval Wales the professional storyteller could, then, on occasion produce a short story which (in spite of its very different technique and style) belonged in essence to the modern

26

genre, and D. J. Williams is the greatest, though not the most obvious or the most prolific, inheritor in the twentieth century of this old tradition. It was a tradition which he would transform, so that today we can recognise that there are two distinct types of short story writer in Welsh, even though their final products may be very similar, and even though the short story first appears as a deliberate literary form in Welsh in the present century. The few earlier examples are casual 'sports' from some other genre— 'The Dream of Rhonabwy' from romance, 'The Biography of Dai Self-important' by Brutus (David Owen) from satire, Daniel Owen's 'The Widow from Aberdare' from the character sketch.

In the twentieth century there is this clear contrast between the work of Richard Hughes Williams (Dic Tryfan) or Kate Roberts on the one hand and that of D. J. Williams or Islwyn Williams on the other. The contrast is not in the settings of the stories: all four writers depict Welsh-speaking communities, and to a large extent communities of the old tradition, but whereas Dic Tryfan and Kate Roberts are consciously working up Welsh raw material according to European literary specifications, D. J. Williams and Islwyn Williams are telling tales of the old kind in such a way that they generate literature of the new kind. A parallel contrast can be seen in the use made in recent years of materials produced in the Welsh woollen mills: some designers have used (for instance) Welsh flannel to make very effective wedding dresses in the cosmopolitan convention, whereas others have started from the 'Welsh costume' convention and refined and lightened it to produce clothes which can be worn in some contemporary contexts.

The contrast in the short story is most clearly visible in a comparison between Kate Roberts and Islwyn Williams. Most of the latter's stories are put in the mouth of a Swansea Valley working man, and almost all of them are tales which could have been told by such a man for their entertainment value; but none of Kate Roberts's stories would have been told by a Caernarvonshire quarryman to his friends. They would seem to have no point or purpose when told to a group of their own characters. And as D. J. Williams grew in literary stature he moved farther and farther away from this 'country tale' type of story; he became more interested in showing why something had happened, though he was still intensely concerned to show effectively how it had happened, and though what had happened might be something which its characters would themselves find interesting enough to talk about. We shall see in due course that even the first volume of D.J.'s stories has at least one story. 'O'er those gloomy hills of darkness' whose value and interest lie in the road to be travelled rather than in the destination reached, but before examining that particular story we shall need to look at the less complex stories which came before it.

Of these others the earliest, 'Geiriau Cred Adyn', whose title is a pun on that of the Welsh translation of Lamennais's PAROLES D'UN CROYANT, is also the slightest, and apart from the verbal shower-bath provided by everything D.J. wrote, it depends so much on its final twist that it would be quite unfair to outline it. More typical of the country tale transformed but still recognisable is 'The Hearse' (called 'Deio'r Swan' in the reprinted STORÏAU'R TIR), whose rather flat characters are nevertheless carved with delicate wit. Those two stories are both based on a single awkward incident; in 'A Man from over the Mountain' and 'A Successful Year', though both stories belong clearly to the same tradition, the central characters are more substantial.

In 'A Man from over the Mountain' Twm was playing truant on the mountain. The schoolmaster sent out four of his classmates to capture him

'and if you don't bring Tom Jones back safe to me as a prisoner of war' (this was at the time of the South African War) 'I won't give a brass farthing for the four of you together'

but when they rushed in on him he escaped into the mist on the bare back of un unbroken pony,

and whenever I think of the familiar line "Away on the mountains wild and bare", Twm and the pony that afternoon come alive to my mind, for that was the last time I saw him to this day.

Twm was brought back to school the next day, but he escaped again, to take service on a farm 'over the mountain', and to be a man from over the mountain for the rest of his life. 'A Successful Year' has been twice translated into English

29

(by Wyn Griffith and by Glyn Jones) so that it
need not be summarised; this story of the contest
between Rachel of Pant y Bril and the dealer who
came to buy her annual calf was written round
a nucleus of fact from D.J.'s boyhood.

The 'country tale' vein crosses the boundary
between Storïau'r Tir Glas and Storïau'r Tir
Coch, and yields its richest ore in the two
earliest stories of the latter collection, 'The
Eunuch' and 'The Heron'. 'The Eunuch' is
especially notable for its opening paragraph,
perhaps the most instantly effective of any story
in Welsh:

*'What is a eunuch?' asked Ifan Acheth Fach in the Sunday
school.*

*'A bullock', answered Lisa Waun 'r Ewig without a
second's hesitation. And that ended the discussion under that
head.*

*So much by the way, for the sake of the ignorant in this
Bible-less age. But we have another eunuch here, namely one
that was once destined to be such, but was saved by a
chimney of ticklish personality. And this was the manner that
it came to pass:*

—and we are then told how the old bachelor
Daniel was persuaded not to have his tomcat
degraded. The story was based on a tale which
D.J. had told in some company with such élan
that he was challenged to write it up for publi-
cation: though he regarded himself as a poor
raconteur, that was rather because he did not
realise that his hearers like his readers could revel
in his digressions and embroideries. From 'The
Eunuch' we can take at random a pair of

30

examples. Daniel had been brought up by his grandmother, who always kept their little cottage in good condition. She

used to whitewash it regularly in spring and autumn, and sometimes oftener if a preaching service came along, or a more respectable funeral than usual were going to pass along the parish road beside it.

And her minister, the Rev. Sinai Thomas, had influenced Daniel greatly. Temperance and chastity were the great virtues to him, and

it was said that the fiery oratory of this reformer had burnt down every inn sign in the seven parishes, and that in the district unchastity had developed into a sort of fine art, known only to two or three specialists. The nearer these were to the altar, the safer their craft was, said the cynic. The minister was a far-sighted man.

So in 'The Eunuch' the country tale gives an opportunity for ironic comment on society, and in 'The Heron' it gives an opportunity for a tribute (equally ironic in a very different way) to the social virtues which were the ground of D.J.'s faith. 'The Heron', like Maupassant's famous 'La Parure', depends on the final twist of realisation that the central character's years of misery, endured for lack of courage to admit to a financial difficulty, were needless. But Gwion's story seems much more credible, and his fears more creditable, than Mathilde's even though his difficulty was created by his own rashness whereas hers was the result of accidentally losing the borrowed jewellery. Mathilde's is the story of a rather sordid attempt to rise above the level of her dull husband to the heights she believes her beauty to deserve, so that it is impossible to avoid a certain feeling that her abasement to a yet lower level is the natural retribution of her own pride Gwion's plan to get his poacher friend's heron stuffed and sold seems at first to be profitable, but as soon as it is launched he comes to believe that to pay the taxidermist would be to spend on that which is not bread the money which his father had scraped together for his university education. The heron becomes a haunting albatross and Gwion flees to the Welsh Guards (in the first World War)—not so much from his creditor as from his own betrayal of the honesty of his home.

V

Though it was not until some of the stories of STORÏAU'R TIR COCH appeared that D.J. could be clearly seen grappling with the problem of contemporary Wales, he had begun to probe beneath the surface of his characters much earlier. Even in 'A Successful Year', where the final twist is the heart of the story, Rachel is not the paper figure which is all that twist would necessarily require. In 'A Shred of Tobacco' there is a final twist of sorts, but hardly one that would appeal to the audience in a bar parlour; the story's significance lies in its revelation of the hasty, conscientious, sincere nature of Ifan, who suffers such remorse at having driven his mare so hard. His remorse is sharpened by fear that the mare may die in foaling, and deepened by his recognition that the danger to the mare has been caused by his obstinacy, and it prevents him from realising that even the obstinacy is the obverse of his determination to stand on his own feet. The facts of the story are evidently adapted from an accident which D.J. had with a mare and cart; the comment on that accident in his autobiography shows more clearly than the story the grounds for Ifan's fear:

But a mare is a wonderfully sensitive creature in this matter. She will foal almost in an instant; or fail, poor thing, and perish. Among my acquaintance when young, and after that, I know of none of the children of the land who ever saw a mare foaling. But I have heard of one or two failing to foal, when no one could help—not the vet or any one . . .

And the character of Ifan is surely drawn from D.J.'s own father.

The central character of 'O'er those gloomy hills of darkness' is more complicated than Ifan, and the story travels a road whose destination is obvious from its first sentence. There would be no need to emphasise that it is not a final condemnation of a story to say that its end is obvious from its beginning, were it not that some critics of D.J.'s last volume of stories made that objection to one of the best stories in the volume—a story to which we shall return later. If the value of a particular story lies in its final twist, there is of course point in such a criticism, but a story whose only value lies in its final twist can hardly stand up to the test of repeated re-reading.

'O'er those gloomy hills of darkness' takes its title from the first line of one of the finest hymns of William Williams of Pantycelyn, and the mention of Pantycelyn in the first sentence of the story tells us at once that at the end of the story Pantycelyn will somehow have led his soul to be still and gaze over those gloomy hills. But the strength of the story lies in its presentation of the storm in Pantycelyn's soul and of the final stilling of the storm—a presentation made peculiarly convincing by the use of the three main characters of the story: Pantycelyn himself; Dic, the *old red cob with the docked tail which he rode on his preaching tours;* and Twm, the ostler who received them at the Pembrokeshire mansion where they spent the night.

34

We are shown the storm first directly through Pantycelyn's meditations over his vain attempt to reconcile the factions in one of the Methodist 'societies' of North Pembrokeshire: the factions united to attack him and left him anxiously probing the motives of his every action on the long weary journey to Llwyngwair. And Llwyngwair was a fair haven for man and beast: it is Dic's meditation on the contrast between that lodging and so many poorer ones which obliquely presents the attraction of the mansion for his master. The

short-cropped pasture spiced with a tang of sea-salt

of which the cob thought so longingly is a parable of the contentment which his rider longed to reach.

The resolution of Pantycelyn's difficulties is presented obliquely too, through Twm the ostler's account, often repeated in the 'society', of the way he himself was converted when Pantycelyn at last appeared at family prayers on the following morning and gave out the hymn which he had just written. We are not told with crude exactness what set his frustrated heart at rest; that we can guess from a few hints in the earlier part of the story and from the lyric which he composed:

> *O'er those gloomy hills of darkness*
> *   Look, my soul, be still and gaze;*
> *All the promises do travail*
> *   With a glorious day of grace:*
> *   Blessed jubil,*
> *   Let thy glorious morning dawn.*

To this one story D.J. appended a note:

This story is based on the tradition that Williams Pantycelyn composed the hymn 'O'er those gloomy hills of darkness' at Llwyngwair Mansion, near Newport in Pembrokeshire, the home of the generous old family of Bowens who were staunch patrons of the Methodist movement in the eighteenth century; . . . Everything else in the story is imaginary.

That last sentence is suggestive. The tradition set D.J.'s imagination working, to get inside Pantycelyn to try to see how he might have come to write a hymn with that particular flavour at that particular place. That was the way his imagination worked: it was not the inventive imagination of the popular novelist who can create incident and plot, but the sympathetic imagination which can think itself into the mind of another person so as to understand the sources of his actions and present them as credible or indeed inevitable.

'O'er those gloomy hills of darkness' was being written at the time of the Bombing School fire, and it would be easy to see in it a symbol or parable of the contemporary situation. Certainly D. J. Williams went through a period of heart-searching as serious as that which he imagined for Pantycelyn, and reached a similar contentment; but if he was at the time of writing conscious of the story's symbolism, he had forgotten it thirty years later, when his preface to the reprint STORÏAU'R TIR implied that the story had been written earlier. But if there was no conscious use of parable in that story, that can hardly be true of some of the later stories. Indeed, the real gravamen of some citicisms of D.J.'s later stories is that they have too obviously ceased to be simply stories, that they have a didactic purpose which makes them artistically disreputable.

D.J. was not much worried by that kind of criticism. He certainly accepted Eric Gill's statement, 'All Art is Propaganda', as a truth: it was not an aspiration, 'All Art *should be* Propaganda', but a statement of fact. Some of those later stories, however, do seem to be rather vulnerable to a charge of conscious striving towards propaganda—even though the critics have sometimes attacked what they thought the politician must have been preaching rather than what the storyteller was in fact saying, and even though the comments of different critics tend to cancel each other out. The complaint which can be made of those few stories is that their technique is not good enough, so that the characters tend to give the impression of having been specially constructed to play the morality parts assigned to them. So they look insincere; instead of being propaganda for the values which their author so unshakeably holds, and to which their characters should give life, they have the tiny, fatal, touch of obviousness. Their propaganda is a pill, recognisable through the jam, where it should have been the delectable fruit growing naturally on a living plant.

The critics in their turn are vulnerable to a serious complaint against their literary competence, for they have far too often been blind to the subtlety of D. J. Williams's technique. The importance of this point will appear after an examination in some detail of three stories from the later period, which differ in structure and in the relation of the 'factual' story to the message it also carries: 'The Court Cupboard', 'Colbo Jones joins up' and 'Ceinwen'.

'The Court Cupboard' (first published in 1939, and accessible in English in the Faber collection of 1959) is written in the third person: it tells of the last hours of Harri Bach—little Harry—the mason,

a piece of the rock from the uplands of the Cothi, that had slipped into the cogs of the modern machine.

Harri has stayed at home while his sister and the rest of the family, with whom he lives in a South Wales valley, have gone to the chapel singing festival, the *Gymanfa Ganu*. But has his nephew, John Hendry, really gone to the Gymanfa? That is just one question which comes to his mind after a long musing over his life. For John Hendry had been the apple of his eye, the focus of a hope that he would do credit to Harri Bach's 'Old District' of Caio; but the night before, Harri had heard John Hendry telling his sister Gwendolen *in English, of course, as usual* that he had failed his college examinations and was going to Bedford to join the R.A.F. So did Harri Bach finally realise that all his ideals—the ideals of the craftsman who built Caio Terrace, and who remembered that

the men of Caio never went to battle against the English long ago . . . without kicking the earth into the air in chunks

meant nothing to John Hendry. Before that, he had looked at the court cupboard, *the only piece of furniture that he owned in the house,*

which

acted as a sort of anchor in the depths, keeping his personality from being shifted by the ebb and flow around him,

and through which,

the very fibre of the hills like himself, he gazed as through a glass into his own heart, and sometimes into the strange distances beyond

—and he had seen that the cupboard was infested with woodworm. The story ends with Harri's realisation that in the cupboard

was his own will, made years before, bequeathing to his nephew, John Hendry, the four houses in Caio Terrace with what little other property he had. Among which was included, by name, the court cupboard.

The story of Colbo Jones (1941) is told by one of his former pupils, who can now say

I'm a J.P. and a county councillor and so on, and these little B.A.'s and M.A.'s come to me now and again to ask for favours:

his language is a *devastating collection of clichés and platitudes, all in character*—the phrase is the late E. Morgan Humphreys's. Jones was a conscientious objector who came as a stopgap teacher to the County School when the J.P. was preparing to sit 'Senior' for the second time, in 1917. He got his nickname by his rash use of a dialect word for *thrash* in a threat to his undisciplined class, and the story is an account of the class's campaign against him. The climax of the campaign was the singing at the beginning of one school period of the words 'Colbo, Colbo, Colbo' repeated again and again to the tune of *God save the King;* this provoked poor Jones into a physical attack on the ringleaders—after which he joined up. And his name was the first on the Roll of Honour at the old school:

'D. J. Jones, B.A., Private: South Wales Borderers: March 17, 1918',—poor Colbo, the only member of the staff who fell in that war.
 And here we are again now, in the middle of another war.

Ceinwen (1949) is the longest and perhaps the most ambitious of D.J.'s stories. Ceinwen is dying, on the first of May, 1943; the story perhaps suggests that she is dying of venereal disease, and since one critic complained that *there is something ingenuous and inexperienced about the author's idea of venereal disease,* it will be just as well to clear that point out of the way. For though the critic may have been literally right, he was literally wrong: it is not at all necessary to the story that Ceinwen's mortal sickness should be venereal, and it would be quite easy to make it clear that it was tubercular. That indeed is what the signs described suggest, and we are never told in so many words what they mean. Perhaps we have to do, not with the natural ingenuousness of the author, but with the contrived ingenuousness which he has found in Ceinwen or in the friend who tells the story.

For this story is set in a double frame. The teller

is Ceinwen's closest friend; on her daughter's
first birthday she received an urgent letter from
Ceinwen and went (of necessity taking the child
with her) to see her on what would soon be her
death-bed. Most of the story is taken up with
Ceinwen's account of what brought her to that
bed; her friend harks back continually to the
past which is needed as background to Ceinwen's
story. That same critic summarised its substance
with convenient crudity:

*The girl who goes to England to work in an arms factory at
the government's orders is sure to get into trouble: instead of
courting a single man, she will be led astray by a married
man, and the end of it all will be to contract venereal disease
and come home to die; and if she had stayed at home, serving
in a café in Aber-rheidol, she would probably have become a
vicar's wife.*

But that is not the point of the story. The end of
the story is obvious enough from the beginning,
but it is comparatively unimportant that Ceinwen is dying: the point of the story is to show
how this high-spirited, sophisticated, attractive
girl, who seemed to her friend to be so strong a
character, could be 'led astray' as she was. She
was intelligent enough to attract the High
Church curate—and to see that if she married
him she could never be her natural self again.
She had the wit to condemn her first job because
she had to

try to look lovely as though I lived on chocolates

and the sense to see, when it came to the point,
that the bus-driver Thomas Thomas was the

right partner for her—although she made fun of him for being shorter than herself and nick-named him (in English too, not in Welsh) Tommy Twice, and told him very sharply that he ought to be Tommy T.T. It was when she found that Tommy had been stolen from her by the land-lady of his R.A.F. billet that she let herself be won by the attractive foreman in her factory, though she knew by then that he was married.

And when Mr Saunders Lewis dismisses Ceinwen as one of D.J.'s good characters, whom he cannot abide because their brains and souls are made of flannel, he does so because he has not recognised that D.J. is writing in character and that the sentimentalism in the picture of Ceinwen is that of her ingenuous friend with her simple delight in her baby daughter, her anxiety for her hus-band in the Army in North Africa, and her admiration for the colourful, exciting Ceinwen of the old days. Colbo Jones is another of Mr Lewis's flannel-brains, and here again the man who tells the story is revealing his own sentimentalism—the most sentimental senti-mentalism of all, that of the hard-headed unsentimental business man. And it is worth while to contrast that J.P.'s attitude towards Colbo with his attitude towards the Head Master under whom Colbo served so indifferently. The Head Master—'the White Waistcoat'—gets no sympathy at all: the future business man could see through the waistcoat at once and all the time. But Colbo was unpredictable: most of his lessons were a pandemonium of indiscipline, but on certain *rare occasions we felt that there was something in this teacher that was in no one else in the school; something we didn't understand. Yes, Colbo was a strange man, when you came to think about him. I'm a business man, of course; and give me the practical man, every time. But I'll say this, honestly: there's been more than one candidate who's got my vote, as a County Councillor, only because I heard the sound of something in him that was like what I heard from Colbo years ago in one of those strange lessons in the County School.*

Even county councillors refuse to fit tidily into white strait-waistcoats: they insist on developing human quirks in their character, for how else could it ever happen that men like D. J. Williams should be appointed to teaching posts? To some readers, not the least of D.J.'s achievements was to project the picture of Colbo Jones through the half-dark lantern of his old pupil.

VI

If there is any reason in the argument put forward in the last section about the significance of D. J. Williams's technique, there is every reason for turning aside at this stage to take a closer look at some of the details of style and technique in his writing. The subject is wide enough for a doctoral dissertation—and serious enough: but let us hope that the dissertation, when it comes, will not be so solemn as to set D.J. turning in his grave.

D.J. himself, in a broadcast discussion with Mr Aneirin Talfan Davies in 1960, spoke of those who

say that I have long complicated sentences occasionally, and that they are so intertwined that it's impossible to unravel them.

He defended himself, because

I have a sort of conscience, a painful one perhaps, which insists on deciding to say the very thing I want to say, no more and no less; and that's what accounts for that complexity often enough, perhaps.

Those sentences themselves illustrate—rather unfairly, being taken from an unscripted discussion—D.J.'s care, *meticulous* care in the correct sense of the word, for saying what he meant; and G. K. Chesterton said long ago that Style is simply saying what you mean.

Perhaps D.J. would have agreed, not only with Chesterton but also with the little girl who was told to think before she spoke and who asked in answer 'How can I tell what I think until I hear what it sounds like?' Emrys ap Iwan's dictum, that thought and language are jointly begotten, certainly did not mean for D.J. that the right language came easily to the birth: he told Mr Talfan Davies that everything he was willing to acknowledge had been re-written at least once, and sometimes five times or more, and his many correspondents will testify that he can hardly have written a single private letter without a little final correcting and polishing before putting it in the post.

At times he perhaps did a little too much of his thinking on paper. But he had worked very assiduously to develop his natural talent for expression, and fortunately we have some explicit statements of principle from him, not only in the discussions with Mr Talfan Davies and Mr Saunders Lewis, but also in adjudications at the National Eisteddfod, between 1937 and 1954. Eisteddfod committees have been slow to recognise the autonomy of literary criticism: for most of them, the one necessary and sufficient condition for appointment to adjudicate a particular genre seems to have been Eisteddfodic success in that genre. Far too many adjudicators appointed on this basis have shown far too clearly that their warbling of native wood-notes wild was no preparation for assessing the beauty of others' singing, but though D. J. Williams was certainly appointed to adjudicate the short stories in 1937 because he had won prizes for short stories in 1934 and 1935, he proved to be a constructive—and instructive—critic.

He must have been a particularly helpful adjudicator to the apprentice storyteller because he gave particular attention to the detail of the craft. The tendency of critic-adjudicators, when they have been appointed, has been to concentrate on broad issues of concept and message and vision, and to eschew examination of the writers' skill in the craft of presenting the concept or message or vision. D.J. always gave full attention to the presentation, partly perhaps because he felt that he lacked inventive imagination, so that (as he once put it) it infuriated him to read a story whose clumsy craftsmanship spoilt an idea which he would have so delighted in presenting with proper skill.

This attention to the detail of craftsmanship was, and still is, particularly necessary for Welsh prose. In his first adjudication, written in Wormwood Scrubs and read for him at the Machynlleth Eisteddfod of 1937 while he was still in prison, D.J. quoted with approval a saying of the poet R. Williams Parry:

Say what you like, boys, I don't see any hope at all for Welsh prose until our writers are ready to spend a whole fortnight trying to shape a perfect sentence of prose, as a poet must do sometimes in shaping the opening line of a sonnet.

Prose, said D.J., had never had in Wales the sort

of recognition that this implied, and only Richard Hughes Williams and Kate Roberts had taken the short story seriously.

For the others it has up to now been something for them to try their hands on before supper.

So his insistence on detail was not pedantry. Adjudicating at Denbigh in 1939 he said of the competitors whom he placed in the second class

It can be said that their chief weakness is weakness, and the second is like unto it, namely mental laziness. Many of them have not taken so much trouble as to re-read their work before sending it in to the competition so as to correct minor faults in accents, spelling, and punctuation. These are details, it's true. But if they did not think it worth while to trouble the least bit about little, simple things like that, it's not likely that any of their sort would make much of an effort after a clear, complete vision of their work in plan, atmosphere, and characters, not to mention the pleasurable pains of trying to shape an occasional sentence that goes dancing under its burden.

The word *dancing* sends us back at once to D.J.'s description of Dafydd 'r Efailfach:

He would see the thing he was describing so much alive before him that his whole democratic vocabulary danced to serve him. And the zest of the dance was revealed in his laughing eye. The master of the dance was that very word which no one could forget.

(And may Dafydd and D.J. forgive the translation *democratic* for *gwerinaidd*—for we have here, packed into one word, a whole philosophy of

47

life. In this particular context the significance of the word can be indicated by saying that it is a compliment to a Welshman to say that he speaks Welsh like a farm worker).

In his own writing, D.J. was always looking for the very word which no one could forget. But his dancing words do not execute a *pas seul*: he was a great choreographer, using with flexible skill every trick of syntax, drawing with sure touch on every source of live vocabulary—taking the speech of the Square Mile as the basis, adding an occasional Biblical word or phrase, borrowing an English word which would comfortably take a Welsh form, quoting from classical Welsh literature, even coining his own new creations. But perhaps his greatest gift is for breathing life into the dead bones of a metaphor and making it join in the dance, which can be illustrated from a single example turning on the use of the word *cefn* (literally *the back*) in the sense of support. When in 'Pwll yr Onnen' he said that the old man at Cilwennau Fowr was 'yn gefen mowr' to the family at Pwll yr Onnen, it was easy enough to translate the sentence by

The old man . . . was a tower of strength to the family as long as he lived.

In that context, spoken by the old man's grandson in his tumbledown cottage, the expression is a cliché, represented accurately enough by an English cliché; but what can the translator do when in 'The Eunuch' D.J. brings the metaphor to life by speaking of Daniel's losing *cefn llydan,*

48

cysgodol ei famgu—the broad, sheltering back of his grandmother?

It is this sort of problem which justifies the argument that D.J.'s work is untranslatable, an argument which can be reinforced by an examination of some of the translated quotations in this essay. To begin with, there are single words and short expressions: how, for instance, shall *bro* and *ardal* and *ardalwyr* be translated? We have made do with *locals* for *ardalwyr,* though D.J. could have claimed to be one of the *ardalwyr* long after he ceased to be a local. He could have spoken without embarrassment to his fellow-ardalwyr of *Yr Hen Ardal:* would 'the Old District' really pass in similar circumstances in England? And 'my old dear countryside' has perhaps a touch of sentimentality which is absent from *fy hen fro annwyl.*

Then there are the quotations or near-quotations. *And this was the manner it came to pass* (on page 30 above) substitutes a biblical archaism for one based on the Welsh of the Mabinogion. The 'familiar line, *"Away on the mountains wild and bare"* ' (page 29) is in fact the original, but the hymn beginning *There were ninety and nine that safely lay,* from which it comes, is by no means as familiar as the Welsh version.

Finally there are D.J.'s feats of ingenuity in syntax. Take the description of society in the Old District (page 10) as the *most blessed in its equality* he had ever known: that is this unfortunate essayist's attempt to convey what D.J. put without the slightest sign of strain into the three words *fwyaf cydradd ddedwydd.* A literal rendering of sorts would be 'most egalitarianly happy', but that is not English and if it were it would do much less than justice to the Welsh. *Dedwydd* is a finer word than *happy:* it lies between *happy* and *blessed,* having the overtones of neither. It suggests more contentment than *happy,* and less religion than *blessed. Cydradd* in turn lacks the conscious, politico-sociological, overtones of *egalitarian;* as a matter of grammar, it needs to be translated by an adverb, but there is no English adverb that will serve.

The description of

the short cropped pasture spiced with a tang of sea-salt

which attracted Pantycelyn's cob (page 35) has no religious or sociological implications; it is purely sensuous, but it presented a teasing problem. The original is

y borfa grop, grop, a min yr heli'n ei flasuso

and though all the words are simple enough, only the first two go simply into English—and we cannot even be sure that they ought not to become 'the grass' rather than 'the pasture'. The doubled adjective *grop, grop* is mutated from the root of the verb borrowed from the English *crop,* but perhaps it may apply to short pasture which has never been cropped. And alas, English knows nothing of the delight of intensifying by repetition, though one can sometimes cheat fairly successfully, as in the translation (page 22) of *yn gynnil, gynnil* by *subtly, very subtly.* The rest of

50

the translation is necessarily even looser. The structure of the Welsh sentence gives 'with the *min* of the *heli* to *blasuso* it'—which would be tolerable English syntax if only the two nouns and the verb could be translated directly by English nouns and verb. But *min* means *lip* or *edge*—including the cutting edge of a blade; *heli* means *brine;* and *blasuso* is the verb made from an adjective meaning *tasty* (and the adjective is quite as hackneyed as the English adjective); and no one of those English words can be used without destroying the atmosphere of the sentence.

To sum up D. J. Williams's craftsmanship we can borrow from his own description of the craftsmanship of Harri Bach:

the craftsmen of the valley still spoke occasionally of the mason's work of Caio Terrace, though they were four perfectly plain houses as far as plan went . . . He admitted quietly to himself that he had never passed the four houses without a loving look at the craftsmanship of the hewn stone of their front and at the pillars of the court before them. Every stone of them was comfortably solid in its place, as though it had been melted there . . . Tonight, when his mind was somehow so unusually lively and clear, he remembered how the chosen stones from the pile slid into their places as though of their own accord, and how he gave each one a tap with the handle of his hammer, by way of blessing as he left it.

Just so would the chosen words from D.J.'s pile slide into their places. And in the next sentence there is a pregnant comparison:

The only experience like it that he sometimes had was in chapel, when his bass voice lost itself in the sea of sound that came from the organ and the congregation, so that he could feel the floor vibrating under him at an occasional note. There was something in experiences like these that tickled the inside of his heart.

There is a sort of parallel here to what D.J. describes as the

odd, strange, effect of great music, music beyond my unmusical comprehension

on him: it could

rouse what creative imagination I have in some other, quite irrelevant, direction. Listening to it, sometimes, I find myself, for example, all unknowing, taking hold again of some limp weak sentences which I have been shaping in the previous days without being at all satisfied with them, and giving them new bones and blood and nerves so that they walk, as they ought to do, on their own feet.

Harri Bach took pride in the way

the rough stones from the Black Mountain had been hewn into polished ashlar under the stroke of his hammer

and D.J. could take the same pride in the detail of his craft.

But (to quote Emrys ap Iwan again)

among men of letters as among craftsmen, it is the skilled architect, not the quarryman, who ranks highest. Good structure is the soul of style, and with that soul style is immortal. A heap of marble stones breaks up and is swiftly lost; but a building of bricks stands for many ages.

In his Machynlleth adjudication D.J. used a similar metaphor:

In style, pebbles from the river appear most often, with hardly ever a strong polished stone as the key of a bridge in the story.

But he himself had worked not only to prepare keystones but to design bridges; he had trained himself in a way which he described in that same adjudication through a parable:

And in the north of Carmarthenshire there was a shoemaker whose name was John. And in those days when ready-made shoes did not fill the walls of the shops, he was the best shoemaker in the land. John the Shoemaker was not the son of a shoemaker, and he was not apprenticed to a shoemaker. But while he was still a lad he took it into his head to unpick old shoes. He tried hard to get hold of old pairs made by the best shoemakers. As he unpicked one shoe after another, stitch by stitch, he took careful and detailed notice of the way they were put together; and in the end he began to make shoes himself. That was how John the Shoemaker came to be the best craftsman in the land.

So in his broadcast discussion with Mr Saunders Lewis D.J. told of critically dissecting hundreds of stories, and he modestly acknowledged the value of some English manuals on the short story. But

for good or ill I never felt any urge to try to follow the pattern of style of any other writer of stories. My constant

*aim was to be as faithful as possible to the people I had met
on the journey of life and to the nation and the society to
which I belonged.*

The previous section of this essay has given a
hint of his success in varying his technique; here
we can follow the hint a little further.

More than half his stories are simple enough in
structure: they are told in the third person by an
omniscient author, and they nearly all start at or
very near the beginning. This is something of a
weakness in the satirical stories of the later
period: those in which the propagandist aim
seems too clear perhaps fall short because they
spend too much time in the preliminary build-up.
'The Court Cupboard' has never been criticised
as propaganda by Welsh speakers (though when
the English translation was first offered to an
Anglo-Welsh periodical the editor could not
stomach the Caio man's revulsion against the
English army); perhaps it is because it starts very
near the end that it carries its satire so much more
effectively.

There are only three stories which are told
directly in the first person, and 'Colbo Jones joins
up' is the only one in which this technical device
has much significance. There it is essential;
indeed, as we have seen, the story is quite as
much that of the J.P. who tells it as that of the
schoolmaster about whom it is told. D.J. Williams
has got inside the J.P.'s improbable skin and seen
that the skin was not wholly impervious: the
schoolboy was really rather ashamed of the
crudity of his companion Ianto Black Ox, as well

as having shrewdly taken the measure of the White Waistcoat and dimly perceived that there was in Colbo something out of the ordinary.

D.J. has used more often the technique of the double remove: as in 'Ceinwen' we are given the ingenuous friend's account of Ceinwen's account of her catastrophe, so in 'Pwll yr Onnen', for instance, the story of that farm is told by a man who heard it as a farm lad over forty years earlier, partly in the words of old Tomos Ifan the Bigws and partly as the lad picked it up from him and from other people in the district. It is a sombre story, in the minor key struck by the first sentence:

It was on a wet October evening that I heard this story; and somehow the clayey dampness of the road home, and the darkness of that night, have clung to it in my mind ever since.

The atmosphere is intensified by the description of the scene of the story:

The farmhouse of Pwll yr Onnen lies in a sort of basin in the midst of a small plateau. On either side of this plateau there are deep wooded valleys, which meet near the bottom of the farm land. From somewhere in these depths is heard the quivering noise of a stream falling as it were into an ever-empty pitcher—a long sound, full of suffering, from which there is no escape . . . From a distance, the cluster of black trees round the house looks like a funeral on a rainy day. Tomos said quite definitely that it used to rain there three days in the week like the clock; and by his grandfather's testimony, if you heard the old boys of Pwll yr Onnen shouting louder than usual, it was a sure sign of a change in the weather.

Those two passages ought to be taken together, for they show why the gloom of the rainy evening started Tomos Ifan off on the story which he had heard

from his grandfather, 'at Cilwennau Fowr, long ago', where he had heard and seen so many of the big things of his life.

So the story goes back—forty years to the farm lad's youth, two generations further to old Tomos's youth, perhaps a generation further to the days of Tomos's grandfather's prime; and we receive it

out of the mouth of two or three witnesses, one behind the other and passing on his evidence,

as C. E. Montague put it in one of the essays in A WRITER'S NOTES ON HIS TRADE.

Montague was speaking in praise of the technique of Kipling and Conrad, and made his point again with a second metaphor:

They say that sherry ought to live for a while in an old brandy-cask, so as to contract a certain convincing quality from the cask's genial timbers. Perhaps the most convincing sherries of all have lived in two successive casks, or in more.

But after that, Montague had his doubts: Jane Austen, Fielding, Scott, Balzac, do not seem to have thought about their technique at all, and he asked

does it arise from something still unexplored, in the very nature of narrative fiction, that its richest and strongest practitioners should look like very standard-bearers of the cause of technical looseness?

Perhaps indeed it does so arise, and perhaps it is not an accident that 'Pwll yr Onnen', in which the successive filters through which the story is passed are not set with strict care to cover each other exactly, is the story which among all D.J.'s work most successfully conveys a particular atmosphere. And certainly we must remember that 'O'er those gloomy hills of darkness', the story which above all the others seems to grow more convincing with re-reading, is the story which fits least smoothly into any definable pattern. Here D.J. has taken complete freedom to change his viewpoint as often as he found it would throw the light he wanted on his central character. There can be no doubt that on occasion he could erect his architectural masterpiece without laying down a recognisable ground plan, and the would-be literary critic is left, rather as Montague was, wondering whether perhaps it is not lost labour to eat the bread of critical carefulness.

VII

All the critical carefulness applied to the technique of D. J. Williams's short stories can be forgotten when we turn to his next work, for there is no difficulty in conveying a fair impression of the technique of HEN DÝ FFARM. It is pure *Tristram Shandy*.

In his broadcast discussion with Mr Saunders Lewis in 1947, D.J. insisted that he was not good at telling stories in company because he was such a poor liar:

When I'm telling a story I find it hard to depart from the literal truth of an event or a saying. A little elastic in the conscience is indispensable to a storyteller, I believe.

He went on to another characteristic which he regarded as a weakness:

I'm under a continual temptation to elaborate on the margin —perhaps a word about the one who told me the story, the occasion, some elaboration about the characters in the story, until the canvas has all unknown to me become too wide before I've reached the point of the story.

Perhaps these weaknesses matter less than he thought. Of course we all know the infuriating person who cannot answer a simple question without a detailed circumstantial introduction— the friend who is sent out, five minutes before the shops shut, to buy cheese for the evening's party, and when he returns an hour later takes a further half-hour to recount his adventures before he can let you know whether he got the cheese or not. From that man, what we really want is cheese, not chit-chat; but if a man is telling us a story, all the digressions may be so many additional strokes in the portrait of the character being presented to us, and in the portrait of the man who is presenting him. John Jenkins of the 'Cart and Horses', whose story-telling D.J. so often quoted, digressed enough in all conscience.

In his short stories D.J. sternly restrained his urge to wander, so that any digressions there may be are deliberately inserted for a purpose; in HEN Dŷ FFARM he let himself go—equally deliberately, no doubt. There is of course a technical reason for this: if a short story writer gives his discursiveness free rein, his story can very quickly lose the unity which enables it to remain in the mind as a single picture. And a feeling that the wider canvas would enable him to tell better the truth as he saw it was certainly one reason for D.J.'s giving up the short story in favour of autobiographical writing. He admitted himself that if the political situation in Wales had not troubled his conscience so that he could not give his first devotion to writing, he would have been likely to turn to the novel. By the time he was writing the stories which would appear in STORÏAU'R TIR DU, that seemed to be the natural direction of his development: he looked like a novelist who had spent years in practising his craft on the smaller scale of the short story and was now ready to take to his real métier.

This would have enabled him to present characters more fully-developed than those of the short
stories, characters shown in the round and
exposed to judgement—loving judgement, indeed, since the novelist must love his creatures,
but without concealing or ignoring their weaknesses. And he could surely have written novels
which, like the greatest serious novels, would
continually tickle the reader's imagination. He
did not write his novels because, as he told Mr
Talfan Davies,

*I felt that I hadn't got enough imagination or enough of a
gift for designing the plot of a story or a novel . . . But I had
so much interest in human nature, its good and evil, that I felt
some sort of spiritual compulsion to portray the characters and
the society in which I've moved all my life. And I think I've
succeeded better . . . through the medium of autobiography
than through the story, or the novel if I'd been venturesome
enough to take on a task of that size.*

If D.J. had accepted the fact that anything in the
way of an orderly plot is no longer essential to
the novel, he might have re-cast the material of
HEN DŶ FFARM and YN CHWECH AR HUGAIN OED
as an autobiographical novel. The novel would
naturally have finished with the loose ends neatly
tied up as the hero, now a conscious nationalist,
entered the University College of Wales; and it
could be a healthy exercise for a bright student
with a taste for literary criticism to plan the outline of that novel—to try out his hand at a
re-orchestration of the material, as it were. But
it would take a genius to carry the work through
beyond the planning, for the existing orches-
tration is the work of a genius using with un-

fettered freedom the themes which had been his inspiration throughout his life.

D.J. spoke of these works as autobiography, but HEN DŶ FFARM can be properly called auto-biography only if it is regarded as the first part of a single two-volume work. So considered, it sets the scene for the more personally-centred second part, in which the static world of the child is replaced by the continually-changing world of the growing boy and the young man. Taken alone, HEN DŶ FFARM is another portrait of the Old District—fuller, looser, more detailed, than HEN WYNEBAU. It is true that D.J. is the starting-point of HEN DŶ FFARM: the first sentence tells of his birth. But he is the starting-point as a stone is the starting-point when it is thrown into a lake, or a puddle. The stone can sink to the bottom and be forgotten: interest concen-trates on the way the waves spread out from the centre created by the stone's impact, the signs they give of the depth of the water or the presence of submerged creatures, the way they strike on rocks or floating objects, what happens when they reach the boundary of the water.

To switch to another metaphor which has been used by some critics, when D.J. has finished with it the Old District is covered by a spider's web of relationships by blood or marriage, but D.J. is not the spider at the centre, and the metaphor is not a happy one, except in so far as it reminds us that in a country district the touching of a thread at any point may awake a very distant spider. We are not expected to carry all the relationships in our mind: D.J. was not compiling a directory but weaving a picture. And to appreciate a woven picture—indeed, to see it at all—one must stand far enough away from it.

That is just as true for the weaver as for the spectator. D.J. had to have the experiences of Yn Chwech ar Hugain Oed before he could see the vision which would make it possible to write Hen Dŷ Ffarm. The social anthropologists, it seems, argue among themselves whether the beehive should be described by the beekeeper or the bee; in Wales the bee seems to be preferred. But the bee has to get outside the hive before he can describe it; indeed, he has to get outside it before he can know that it is a hive at all. So D.J. spent many years gathering honey and other more bitter substances in the draughty world outside before he consciously recognised how warm the community of the hive was.

Hen Dŷ Ffarm covers only six years of D.J.'s life: like Tristram Shandy, D.J. had to follow up so many threads as he went along that he could not progress fast. And the title of the book is no accident, for if it covers only six years of D.J.'s life it covers sixty years of Penrhiw, the 'old farmhouse' where he was born, and it sets even that period in the context of his family's occupation of Llywele, the home of the Iberian tribe of the Old District, since the fifteenth century. But we hear nothing to speak of about Penrhiw until the second chapter: the first chapter—the first of the four movements of the symphony— is a series of loosely related variations on the theme of the memory of a child. There was only one event in D.J.'s early life to which he could give a definite date—the move from Penrhiw to Abernant when he was six and a quarter; but he could set his memories of earlier events exactly in the place where they occurred, and tell in whose company he was at the time.

So,

like turning on a tap when the water is under high pressure, a flood of reminiscences comes to me, if I give it a chance, memories of little trivial incidents.

And in this way he remembered an occasional journey with his mother to Llandeilo market; and since the journey was made in the trap drawn by the faithful Blac, there is at once a digression about horses. There are further digressions about the carriers on the road, about the relatives who lived in farms within sight, and then Llandeilo town and its market are placed in their relation to the Old District. Llandeilo, like Lampeter and Llanybydder, was a homely familiar place, whereas Carmarthen, with its English assize judge, its jail, and its Mayor (the Mayor of Carmarthen was the object of a superstitious awe which made 'cursing the Mayor on the top of Alltwalis Hill' a proverbial expression for bravery in the absence of danger) had

a feeling of distance, of wonder, and of strangeness

which D.J. connected with his father's

hatred of an Englishman's tyranny and arrogance [which] was carried to an unreasonable pitch

though

if an English tramp came by he would share his ration of tobacco with him as generously as he did with any Welshman who was dying for a smoke.

John Jenkins, too, contributed to this educative process,

and in that way, before ever I crossed the school threshold, I began to learn the history and geography of Carmarthenshire, learning much of it on the spot by my mother's side on the seat of the trap, listening to her speak of people and houses and woods and fields, of stream and river and lake that we saw on that romantic and brightly coloured twenty miles on those occasional journeys between Llandeilo and Lampeter, and, when I was a little older, when listening to John Jenkins, as much, perhaps, as anyone, with his stories of the big wide world beyond our horizon.

The second chapter is entitled 'Aelwyd Penrhiw yn Amser fy Nhadcu' and the translator has wisely expanded the literal translation of *aelwyd* from *hearth* to *hearth and home*. The chapter in fact covers much more than even that suggests, for it explains how the grandfather came to leave the ancestral home at Llywele after a disagreement with his landlord's agent. It goes on to show that there was a basis of truth in the family tradition that the line of the Llywele tenants was related to that of their landlords at Edwinsford: in this context it will be appropriate to use the snobbish English misrendering of *Rhydodyn*—the Welsh name which seems to mean 'the kiln ford', and which has been kept in the English translation of HEN DŶ FFARM. But the Edwinsford line had been able to take advantage of the introduction of English land law to Wales, and none of D.J.'s relatives ever spoke of his belief in the family connection, lest

he might be suspected of inclining to the same mental condition as poor Harris Cathilas

who had swallowed the tradition

so completely that he became deranged and developed the phantasy that some of the farms on the Rhydodyn estate belonged to him.

D.J. never knew his grandfather, who died when he was less than a year old, but during that last year of the old man's life

my mother nursed him, in the heavy oak cupboard bed in the parlour, with the same tender hand as she nursed his little grandson in the cradle on the floor under the big chimney mantel. When he got up sometimes to the hearth, so I heard it said, he spent much of his time over the cradle, amusing and talking to the two most constant occupiers of that corner, myself and Twm the cat.

But the core of the chapter is the tale it tells of the grandfather's pioneering at Penrhiw, a tale pointed with stories which may, by the time D.J. came to write them down, have had little enough resemblance to the original bald facts. For

in commemorating Penrhiw in my grandfather's time I have sometimes two or three versions of the same story to compare and to choose from: my father's plain but slightly varying version, Uncle Josi's classical one with every cough and huh huh in its right place, and also the highly coloured

65

and romancing version given by the two men who were in service there in turn for a period of several years. This last version, after going from mouth to mouth in the locality for a long time, is not always easy to reconcile with the others.

And though

it was indeed hard work and a hard life in Penrhiw in the old days . . . the stories I heard about it are so many that I should think there was some bit of innocent fun on the go every day amid the high spirits,

and

despite many disadvantages that might be noted of living in a place like Penrhiw, there must have been outweighing advantages

which kept gifted young men like those two tellers of tales in service there for years.

This second movement of the symphony ends with a dying fall:

during the forty-six years my grandfather was [at Penrhiw], from Michaelmas 1840 till his death in May 1886 at the age of seventy-eight . . . the place went through a transformation. . . . The valleys were cleared of their pristine wild growth, and woods were planted neatly and skilfully by the method of mattock and line, and the thick-skinned lay land was turned into green fields between banks with sheltering hedges that showed the work of spade and bill-hook. Under his industrious hand hilly inaccessible Penrhiw became one of the best-conditioned, most progressive, and most productive farms in the vicinity. . . . the marks of the old man's labour and planning are still to be seen there in many places. In a vague but subtle manner the influence of his spirit is felt to some degree to this day by at least one of his grandsons. There are great-grandsons and great-grandsons' children living not far from this old homestead who do not know that such a man ever existed. It appears that it was not in vain after all that my grandfather shared his love and attention in his last days between Twm the cat and that grandson of his.

The third movement, 'Penrhiw Hearth and Home in my Time' (in which the stories are told from D.J.'s own memory of them), and the fourth, 'Leaving Penrhiw', have rather similar concluding passages. The last movement spoils the symphonic comparison by being in a minor key: the chapter is shadowed by the anxiety of D.J.'s parents. The father's recurring ill-health made it impossible for him to supervise the work at Penrhiw, and his bachelor younger brother (*Uncle Jâms* to D.J.), who lived with the family, was a broken reed. He would try to take the lead, and succeed only in upsetting everything and everybody, and especially his sister-in-law. She had patience for everything except his special kind of obstinacy, and it was the impossibility of life at Penrhiw which led to the move to a smallholding which she and her ailing husband could work alone. But the movement and the symphony end with a sweetened melancholy in the description of the evening of the move to Abernant:

Later that day there was a sort of Merry Evening in Abernant, to warm the hearth: hymn-singing and the singing of old eisteddfod pieces—Tomos Hafod Wen (John Thomas's predecessor there), one of the gentlest persons there ever were, and my father with him singing tenor like two flutes, Benni the Shoemaker with his bass notes like an organ beneath his beard-hidden breast; and the broad-chested baron Uncle Josi with his polished mabinogi was there somewhere, not to speak of the neighbours young and old. But the last and most prominent thing that has remained in my memory, before going to bed that night, was Uncle Jâms leaning back on the nape of his neck against the wall under the chimney mantel, with his eyes quite shut, completely lost in the delight of the splendid old melody 'Hobed o Hilion' . . . On the solid oak chair by the big clock near the dairy door sat old grey-bearded William Thomas the Carpenter, Llansewyl, and the bright head of the hammer in his hand beat the time on the grey brick at his feet. The welcome must have been warm, for the cracks made in that brick that night are to be seen to-day.

In that desperate effort to convey the impression of D. J. Williams's writing, we may try yet another comparison as we pass from HEN Dŷ FFARM to YN CHWECH AR HUGAIN OED. HEN DŷFFARM has a spiral shape. The story starts from D.J. himself at the centre, but at once runs out to a distant circumference, and then goes round and round in ever-decreasing circles, until at the end it reaches the centre again. YN CHWECH AR HUGAIN OED is much less discursive—after all, it covers twenty years of D.J.'s life where HEN Dŷ FFARM covers only six—and at times it moves forward quite fast. But its progress is rather like that of a man taking a walk with a dog: the man moves steadily forward, and the dog moves forward too, but with a perpetual irregular oscillation in any and every direction.

The vision of the spiral can be pushed a little further: let us think of it as a three-dimensional figure made of strong wire, and see the rising

68

turns of the narrowing spiral making a handle, until the centre is reached and the wire turns sharply along the axis of the spiral to form a dart which pierces to the truth about D.J. After all the preparation, he has reached a new nest, as secure and cosy as the old one, and the 'Merry Evening' —the sing-song round the hearth —gives hope of a joyous future to come. In the first two chapters of YN CHWECH AR HUGAIN OED we are told how the hope was fulfilled in the ten sociable years which followed.

They were years more sociable than those at Penrhiw because as the boy grew he could venture further afield, but much more because Abernant stood by the road along which everyone passed from Rhydcymerau towards the great village of Llansawel ('as a *village,* probably the biggest village in the world', as one of its sons boasted to the envious D.J.) and the great world beyond that. At sixteen, D.J. would be going out into that great world, but at six the new home was world enough:

If I had at some time to make a list of the happiest periods— I might almost say the most ecstatic periods—I have experienced in my life, I would have to include among the chief of them those first days when we came as a family to live in our new home at Abernant, in the middle of October 1891; my first weeks at Oxford in the same month of 1916 . . . with the three weeks of splendid holiday which I spent in Vienna in August 1923.

His roots were at Penrhiw, and at Llywele before it, but Abernant was the centre of his Square Mile.

69

Here then with his younger sister Pegi he played the gentleman farmer with their cattle and horses,

all brought into being by me, with the help of imagination and my father's pocket-knife, from the hazel and birch, ash and willow of the hedges alongside, and according to a strict convention understood by specialists alone.

They had no pigs or poultry on their farm; those were

things too common for gentleman farmers to bother with;

and they needed no wooden dogs, for Mac the Quick-witted Dog and Dash the Half-witted Dog (those translations will have to do for *Ci Call* and *Ci Hanercall*)

were always at hand in the flesh.

And so in due course when they were about ten,

the yoke of the ordinary farmer descended gently and un-noticed on our young shoulders.

It was a yoke which D.J. was glad to bear. He resisted his mother's encouragement to go to Llandeilo County School at the age of twelve:

horses working on the land, and the company of fellow-workers, old and young, were my whole delight.

So he left school at thirteen and worked on the land for three years—years on which he looked back as the silliest period of his life, marred by *trifling, Uncle-Jâms-like obstinacy, and needless, provoking, venturesomeness*

but never by laziness or slackness about anything. By the time he was sixteen he had made himself a reputation as a country poet—but a poet who was such a dangerous satirist that many of the neighbours were glad to see the back of him as he set off for the Rhondda.

The third chapter of Yn Chwech ar Hugain Oed, 'At the Coal Face', is the kernel of the book. It takes up nearly half of it, but more important than its extent is its significance, for it was while he was working underground that D. J. Williams came to recognise his roots, though he himself never made this explicit. It was from the darkness of the coal-mine that the bee first caught sight of the hive, but the title of the last chapter, 'Gwyrdroi Breuddwyd', suggests an incomplete realisation of what had been happening, whether we translate it 'A Dream Perverted', or more mildly 'A Dream Turned Aside'. For surely the truth is that the dream was something of a nightmare.

According to D.J.'s own account, his aim when he went to work underground was to earn good money and save enough to go to America to farm, and since he did earn good money and save much of it, he would have gone to America at the age of 21 if his uncle, his mother's half-brother, had not stayed in Carmarthenshire instead of returning to Kansas and taking D.J. with him.

71

Providence interfered. And the result of that interference is that I'm writing this book as it is now, instead of telling my story as the Buffalo Horn King or something great and American of that sort; or, much more probably, soliloquising as a little old man trimming a hedge somewhere on the edge of the Rocky Mountains, in some little combe that would be wonderfully like Cwm Pant 'r Onnen, alongside our house at Abernant long ago, as I used to see it at the end of the last century.

It was Providence which turned the nightmare aside in 1906, but in 1902 it was a glorious dream:

My deepest instincts had not yet awakened in me, and I never conceived that circumstances would one day interfere, and keep me from breaking my destined attachment to the land of my fathers.

D.J. left home, partly because of the American dream; partly because his verse had made the Old District a little warm for him; but most because Abernant was really too small a farm to provide a living for one man, let alone two. And

as in every country district, most of the Old District's children, generation after generation of them, were scattered in every direction to look for a living

—and, surely, to look at a little of the world.

So in January 1902 D.J. started before dawn one day, to catch the train at Llandeilo and travel to the Rhondda. As he left Abernant he noticed once again the hedge which their neighbour had recently laid with such skill; when he reached the Rhondda, he was astonished

72

*to see, after coming through the Blaengwynfi tunnel to the top
of the Rhondda Fawr, how close together all these important
places were. There you were, Blaenrhondda, Treherbert,
Treorchy, Cwmparc, Pentre, Tonypandy, Trealaw, Llwyny-
pia, Dinas, all in a row down to Porth where the two valleys
met, and then back on the left up the Rhondda Fach—
Ynyshir, Pontygwaith, Tylorstown, Ferndale where I was
going now, and Maerdy at the head of the valley—all
almost joining up with each other, with hardly more room
between them than between so many farms up there with us
in Carmarthenshire—from Bwlch Cae Melwas down to
Rhydodyn bridge and back again on the left, up the Cothi to
Crugybar or Caio village.*

D.J. had gone to Ferndale because his cousin John
was already working there, and at first they
lodged in the same house; but the family connection soon slackened, for the cousins' tempera-
ments were very different. John was driven by an
ambition which sent him farther and farther
west, to become in the end a Government land
surveyor in British Columbia, but D.J. was
able to settle in contentedly in the mixed
community of the Rhondda and to get to know
it in all the rich variety of its interests, from
boxing to Welsh verse (but seldom to revivalist
meetings), and at the same time to do a man's
work while he was still a growing lad.

The Rhondda was still

three-quarters Welsh in spirit, in language and in culture

when D.J. worked there; there was a Welsh
bookshop on the Square at Ferndale—but the
picture one carries away from his account is of a

society already cosmopolitan and of a hurried life, almost frenzied in its activity, in the greatest contrast with the leisurely rhythm set by the seasons for the farming society of the Old District. And though he speaks favourably of the society above ground, it is clear that he found his companions underground more congenial than most of his fellow-lodgers, and that reading, rather than any more social interest, was his chief spare-time activity. His most memorable pictures from this period are from the mine.

So though he was happy enough at Ferndale and certainly not homesick (he took only one holiday at home during his two and three-quarter years there), he had no idea of staying there for ever. Nevertheless, this is the really significant part of his industrial career: the two periods at Betws and Seven Sisters are mere appendices. In the Amman Valley he found himself in a society that was still half rural, and included a substantial colony of emigrants from the Old District. He lodged with one of the emigrants—a slightly older contemporary from the next farm to Abernant, who had just settled in after marrying a wife from one of the Three Tribes. But he was not to have a long stay in this transplanted homeland; he did not get on well with the under-manager who had come down from Lancashire with the company which ran the mine, and when a dispute over wages led to a lock-out, he moved again, to the Dulais Valley, and after a further nine months he went home to Abernant, all set for the great journey to America.

But 'Providence intervened'. The uncle from America postponed his return there, and the hold of the American dream was not strong enough to make D.J. venture there alone; it was abandoned for ever after the uncle married and settled down in Pencader. D.J.'s deteriorating eyesight kept him from returning to the mine, and he was persuaded to spend the winter at Stephens's school at Llanybydder, one of the private ventures which catered for the mature student, who was usually preparing for the ministry. D.J.'s stimulus was less specific; he had a

vague desire, deep down, for more education and learning for their own sake,

and having once taken up his school books he went on for five years until he entered the University College of Wales in 1911.

The road to Aberystwyth was not direct. It led through correspondence courses and examinations, and a period at another private school, that of the Rev. Joseph Harry at Carmarthen, who is the subject of one of D.J.'s neatest character portraits. And it led to Llandrillo in Merioneth, where he served as an uncertificated teacher for two years. He had a religious experience there, a conversion following an unhappy love affair, which he used in a story not reprinted in STORÏAU'R TIR. But he had other experiences there which were spiritual though not religious, for Llandrillo was consecrated ground. It was only a dozen miles from Llanuwchllyn, the home of Sir Owen Edwards, whose periodicals were the purest channel of Welsh culture in those days;

they had been inspiring D.J. since he first saw a copy of 'the red *Cymru*' at the age of fifteen.

And at Llandrillo he came to full realisation of the instincts which had not awakened when he began to dream of America: now he really saw Wales as a true unity. It is not an accident that the political gospel is most often proclaimed in this chapter, to the embarrassment of so many Welsh readers. But it must be left to a different generation to decide whether our embarrassment can be defended or excused, for in one way or another we of this generation are all too closely involved. To some of us, D.J. seems to be knocking too insistently at an open door; to all of us, perhaps, his voice is a disturbing reminder that our practice falls short of our profession. The longest political passage contrasts the Welsh attitude towards nationhood with that of other countries, and starts from a declaration of D.J.'s own vision of national unity:

As a man from the South who was for some two years a member of a rural and really cultured society in North Wales, and who moreover had for over thirty years the privilege through Plaid Cymru—the only Welsh political party since the days of Owain Glyn Dŵr—of associating closely with a pretty good number of the people of the North as well as the South, it would be easy for me to succumb to the temptation to pontificate about the differences between South and North, difference in dialect, in temperament and character, as well as in the kind of humour and personal response which springs from those. But at bottom there is in Wales one nation, though it is of mixed blood like every other nation, with all the elements in its destiny and history, since the time before history, woven together into one colourful indissoluble

76

pattern. *The differences are only parts of the glory of that variety which enriches the whole.*

He had described the vision as he saw it on his first journey to the north, to take up his post at Llandrillo:

From Dovey Junction on towards Towyn and Barmouth I had the compartment to myself; and from one point of view that was just as well. For on that day in early October that year all the colours of Nature on land and sea, in all her magic, were around me, and changing under sunshine and cloud almost every other minute. And there was I like a man out of his mind, bouncing from one window to the window on the other side so as not to lose a single flash of the wonderful wealth of light and splendour on sea and land on every side. In later years I was to see the mountains of the Alps and the Tyrol and the glory of the valleys of the Rhine and the Danube, and to be deeply touched by them. But in the world of Nature I have never seen anything that so overwhelmed me as that journey for the first time, from Aberystwyth by Aberdyfi and the mouth of the Mawddach, and up under the shadow of Cader Idris to Dolgellau and the valley of the Wnion, and over the Garneddwen and down to Llanuwchllyn, where I saw the reflection of the Aran and Berwyn in the clear water of Bala Lake, and finally reached the peaceful plain of Llandrillo in the middle Dee Valley. I felt that all these belonged to me. The red Cymru had given them to me as everlasting treasures in my heart; and it had not said a a word too much about any of them.

VIII

In that same volume C. E. Montague has an essay 'Quotation' in which he looks at the way different writers quote, and asks how it comes about that some can use their quotations to such purpose:

Thackeray seems to have been about as idle a dog as the Charterhouse and Trinity have ever essayed to educate, and yet his writing leaves an irresistible impression of French and classical scholarship,

and goes on to offer an explanation:

To be amused by what you read—that is the great spring of happy quotations. Apart from professional writers, run your mind over those of your friends who have been offered the conventional 'good education' of public school and university. One obvious difference among them is between those who worked and those who didn't, those who accepted the offer and those who rejected it. But another and more vital difference is between those who were tickled by what they studied or neglected and those who, studious or not, were not tickled in the slightest. The former might be arrant idlers, and yet you will find them, at forty or fifty years old, making the aptest or most diverting applications of classical tags to common life and public affairs. The untickled may have won any number of scholarships and first classes but before they are thirty they are as dead to what they read in their youth as they are to the trousers in which they read it.

It may be that when all is said and done that is the simple truth about D. J. Williams. He could quote with such effect (from other classics than those of which Montague was thinking) because he had been tickled by them; but he could describe men and animals so vividly because he had been tickled by them too. That is why no one was ordinary when D.J. had finished describing him.

His readers, however, tend to pick and choose among his characters. Some are put off by his satirical pictures: for them, when Sunny Jim Williams took to ploughing the Black Earth, he was committing the blunder of the clown who wants to play Hamlet. Mr Saunders Lewis cannot stand his 'good' characters; for him, D.J.'s genius is for depicting humbugs, and those good people have minds made of flannel. Well, of course, so they have: good people all too often do, and that makes the rest of us very uncomfortable. But Mr Lewis's discomfort ought not to have blinded him to the skill of D.J.'s presentation of those good characters—in character.

Perhaps, however, Mr Lewis must be forgiven, on the ground of a sort of invincible ignorance, an irremovable blind spot on his highly sensitive critical retina. Those good characters of D.J.'s are all Puritans of a sort, and Mr Lewis has so reacted against his Bible-black Methodist-clerical background that he is an undiscriminating Puritanophobe. And yet so perceptive a critic could have been expected to recognise that a very large part of HEN WYNEBAU and HEN DŶ FFARM is really about D.J.'s Puritanism. What it meant can be seen in a paragraph of HEN DŶ FFARM:

Before I went to school or ever was charged, as far as I

remember, in any moral commandments, except never on any
account to say 'No, I won't' to my parents and never to tell a
lie, I believe that somewhere in the depth of my being, and in
a vague and obscure way, I learnt some of the more sacred and
fundamental principles of my life ever afterwards. A
narrow and puritanical home, you say. Not at all. Two
children were never given a healthier ungrudged freedom at
home than my sister Pegi and I. There were one or two
handrails, made by family life, that we were not allowed to
climb over. Near as the devil was to my elbow in my early
days (and worse luck he is quite as near still in another
get-up), and ready as he always was to show a lively and
willing enough servant the work he might do, yet when it
came to a debate between us near these handrails his majesty
had to draw in his tail. And no one could destroy the virtue
and strength of the handrails except myself. And I have
always felt that if my respect for them failed every value
there might be in my life would fail too. Here, in this
simple home, were set up my ideas of religion, of education,
of country and of language and of life, and that before any
of these abstract terms could mean anything to my under-
standing. It was a matter of atmosphere and tradition that had
come down from generation to generation.

D.J.'s Puritanism was this inherited tradition of
the Square Mile, and the contrast between this
natural Puritanism of self-restraint and the
recognition of objective values, which D.J. had
thus inherited, and the killjoy repressiveness
towards others which most of us mean by
Puritanism, lies behind the cross-purposes at
which D.J. and Mr Aneirin Talfan Davies dis-
cussed the 'Welsh way of life'. Mr Davies had asked
D.J. to say what he understood by this, and had
been told that

to define the Welsh way or the English or French way or any

80

other national way of life is as impossible, I would say, as to define the scent of flowers: you see the flowers, and you know the difference between the scent of one flower and the other.

But, said Mr Davies,

to many people without your rural background, the Welsh way of life has become synonymous with certain prohibitions, connected with Sunday, connected with the public-house, connected with this and that

—whereas D.J. had said that

there's no inconsistency at all between the inn and the society around and the chapel in the country; . . . the inn is as much a part of the particular society as the shop and the smithy and so on;

and for him it was the need to re-create a Welsh way of life in an urban society that made a Welsh national government essential. He wanted to see, in an urban setting, a society that was as couth as that of the Old District.

At another level, one element in the couthness of the Old District was respect for others, and for a writer that implies understanding others, getting inside them. This means that a real living character in fiction, a 'round' figure, cannot be a figure of fun—or of whole-hearted hatred. That is the essential difference between D.J. and Caradoc Evans, for the raw material of their stories is at bottom very much the same. The underlying facts of a Caradoc Evans story could often be re-cast into a story in the manner of D.J., but the effect of the new story would be quite different from the original because D.J. would have understood and delineated in the round the person whom Caradoc could only see on the surface and caricature. As written by Caradoc, 'Be This her Memorial' (whose elderly unheroine lived on roast rats so that she could present the young minister with a fine Bible) is a horrid tale; as written by D.J. it would have had a macabre glory. And what would not Caradoc have made of 'The Eunuch'?

It may be argued that Caradoc is describing a different society from D.J.'s—the harsher society of marginal farms, like that of Simon and Beca (in 'The Way of the Earth'), who *were waiting for death* as they saw the ten acres which they had tamed into the most fruitful soil in the district going back to heatherland. But was not Rachel's Pant y Bril (in 'A Successful Year') a pretty marginal holding, and had not Penrhiw itself been marginal land until D.J.'s grandfather bullied it into farmhood? If Caradoc was describing a different society, that was because he saw a different society, and perhaps he saw a different society because he was a different man. He sprayed his particular hive with insecticide because when he had once got outside it he realised that he was a hornet.

Whether or not D.J.'s Square Mile was really richer in honey than Caradoc Evans's, there can be no doubt that D.J. was a bee who recognised all the other occupants of his hive as fellow-bees. That is the true explanation of the apparent inconsistency between D.J.'s picture of the Old

District and the picture drawn by Gwenallt, who was the son of two emigrants from there, brought up in the Swansea Valley and spending holidays on the farms of his relatives back home. According to Gwenallt, Dr Kate Roberts had been misled by a picture which gave too much prominence to those prosperous farms Penrhiw and Abernant; that was why she wrote in a review of HEN DŷFFARM:

Because of this plenty, none of those things happen which we associate with poverty. It's true that some of the family die of consumption, but I can't for a moment think that this was the result of poverty. And we do not have the great dispersing of families because of the migration of many of them to work in the industrial areas. A few go (but not many), perhaps rather in the way of adventure.

Gwenallt quite rightly says that Dr Roberts had a false impression; it is in fact an impression which should have been corrected from the account of the Three Tribes in HEN WYNEBAU, and by the time Gwenallt was writing (in 1965) D.J. had shown clearly how much migration there was from the Old District.

He had shown also how little basis there was for Gwenallt's view that Abernant was a prosperous farm: it was a place small enough for D.J.'s mother to manage alone, if her husband's ill-health made that necessary, and the family had to use every opportunity to get income from other sources. D.J.'s father did not take to doing odd carrying jobs and breaking roadstones for the sake of his health. The truth of the matter seems to be, not that the Old District was particularly prosperous or rich in worldly goods, but that it had no obvious extremes of wealth or poverty, and no class distinctions that were visible to the young D.J.

Perhaps it could be shown that he had a false impression of the social structure when he wrote of the

wonderfully rich world into which I was born, a world in which there was very little anxiety about money, beyond paying the way fairly comfortably without running into debt anywhere, and a world too, as far as I am able to judge, where all, in proportion to their age and experience, were as equal as any human community can be expected to be.

He was certainly speaking with authority when he said of his father

I think he was always on good terms with his Creator. I know he was on the best terms possible with his neighbours, every hour of the day and every day of the year. That was a part of the secret of the life of the Old District.

It was surely true that there people did not have inequality and injustice daily thrust on their attention as they did in the mining valleys of the south and the quarrying uplands of the north.

So there was no sourness or bitterness within the hive: that was reserved for the oppressors from outside. The monoglot English exciseman, the keeper who came trespassing in search of pheasants' eggs, the scoundrelly solicitor, all had their headquarters in the fatter lands lower down the valley. That was where D.J.'s father got the wholly unreasoning hatred of the opulence of the Englishman and of 'those old bigwigs' to which his son more than once referred as having helped to make him a nationalist before he was born.

That hatred, the negative side of his nationalism, was less important than the positive side, the vision of the couth society of the Old District as an incarnation of the essential Welsh way of life —but only one incarnation among many possible ones. Those who praise D.J.'s writing are depressingly ready to speak of it as presenting 'an unforgettable picture of a way of life which has disappeared for ever'—but if some of the forms which the way of life took have disappeared, they are only the accidents, and there is no *a priori* reason why the substance should not remain, as strong as ever, under other forms. The University way of life at Cambridge did not disappear because baths and electric light were put in at colleges, or because chemists and biologists were elected to fellowships, and the Welsh way of life did not disappear because the horse replaced the ox in the plough, or because the threshing machine replaced the flail; nor has it disappeared because the tractor has replaced the horse. But the University way will disappear if dons cease to regard undergraduates as the most important members of the University and if students wage a class war on dons; and the Welsh way of life will disappear if all the Welsh come to hate the language and to despise such craftsmanship as that of Harri Bach in stone and D. J. Williams in words.

That craftsmanship, and the integrity of which it is an expression, are what I think D.J.'s vision meant, though he never stated it in quite such terms as those. He took to political activity because he saw his vision in danger, and he brought to the routine drudgery of his politics the same integrity and devoted commitment as he gave to everything he took up—though Welsh politics was for him the body of death from which he would have given anything, short of that integrity, to be delivered. Yet I cannot believe that he can really have felt Gwenallt's great sonnet to Wales as part of his own experience. He could accept the bitter picture of the nation's degradation:

The cancer is shrivelling thy whole countenance and shape,
There are abscesses and scabs on thy soul,
Thou art nothing but a nightmare in thine own country,

but the opening lines of the sonnet speak the language of a nationalism less inborn than D.J.'s:

Why hast thou given us this sorrow,
And the pain like a lead weight on our flesh and blood?
Thy language like a burden on our shoulders,
Thy traditions fetters on our feet?

The burden was one under which D.J. delighted to dance, and by the traditions his feet were shod with the preparation of the gospel of peace.

After the bitter complaint the sonnet changes its tone:

86

And yet, we cannot leave thee in the mire,
Victim to the mockery and derision of this generation,
Thy freedom of yore is a sword ready to hand,
With thy dignity we shield our breast,
And we take hold of our spears and spur on our horses,
Lest we bring shame on our forefathers in their graves.

D.J. had never laid down his spear; he called to battle on so many pages of his work that many of us feel put to shame; but he did so, not for the sake of the dead fathers, but for the sake of the living nation. She was still the king's daughter, and his vision was clear enough to see that under her muddy rags she was still glorious within.

Select Bibliography

(A full bibliography is appended to D. J. WILLIAMS: CYFROL DEYRNGED (ed. J. Gwyn Griffiths, 1965), with a supplement in Y GASEG DDU A GWEITHIAU ERAILL (ed. J. Gwyn Griffiths, 1970). These bibliographies do not include all the English translations of D. J. Williams's stories, nor the posthumous 'Saunders Lewis—A Man of Destiny' in PRESENTING SAUNDERS LEWIS (ed. Alun R. Jones and Gwyn Thomas; Cardiff, University of Wales Press, 1973).)

BOOKS BY D. J. WILLIAMS

A.E. A CHYMRU. Aberystwyth, Gwasg Aberystwyth, 1929.

HEN WYNEBAU. Aberystwyth, Gwasg Aberystwyth, 1934.

STORÏAU'R TIR GLAS. Aberystwyth, Gwasg Aberystwyth, 1936.

STORÏAU'R TIR COCH. Aberystwyth, Gwasg Aberystwyth, 1941.

STORÏAU'R TIR DU. Aberystwyth, Gwasg Aberystwyth, 1949.

HEN DŶ FFARM. Aberystwyth, Gwasg Aberystwyth, 1953.

MAZZINI, CENEDLAETHOLWR, GWELEDYDD, GWLEIDYDD [Mazzini, nationalist, seer, statesman]. Cardiff, Plaid Cymru, 1954.

YN CHWECH AR HUGAIN OED. Aberystwyth, Gwasg Aberystwyth, 1959.

DETHOLIAD O STORÏAU'R TIR [a selection from the three volumes of short stories, with a short introduction]. Llandysul, Gwasg Gomer, 1966.

CODI'R FANER [Raising the Flag: memories of Plaid Cymru]. Cardiff, Plaid Cymru, 1968.

Y GASEG DDU A GWEITHIAU ERAILL [The Black Mare and other works: early stories and miscellaneous writings, edited by J. Gwyn Griffiths]. Llandysul, Gwasg Gomer, 1970.

TRANSLATIONS BY D. J. WILLIAMS

WYNWNS SIEW [Prize Onions, by E. Eynon Evans]. Aberdare, Stephens and George, 1941.

Y BOD CENHEDLIG [The National Being, by G. W. Russell, 'A.E.', with an introduction]. Cardiff, Plaid Cymru, 1963.

TRANSLATIONS OF WORKS BY D. J. WILLIAMS

'A Good Year' ['Blwyddyn Lwyddiannus'], translated by Wyn Griffith: in WELSH SHORT STORIES (London, Faber, 1937), pp. 373–80, and TWENTY-

FIVE WELSH SHORT STORIES (ed. Gwyn Jones and Islwyn Ffowc Elis; Oxford Paperbacks, 1971), pp. 225–9.

'Pwll yr Onnen', translated by Dafydd Jenkins: in WELSH SHORT STORIES (selected by Gwyn Jones; Harmondsworth, Penguin Books, 1940), pp. 157–65, and WELSH SHORT STORIES (selected and introduced by Gwyn Jones; World's Classics, 1956), pp. 313–22.

'The Court Cupboard' ['Y Cwpwrdd Tridarn'], translated by Dafydd Jenkins: in WALES (ed. Keidrych Rhys), vol. v, pp. 74–81 (1945), and WELSH SHORT STORIES (ed. George Ewart Evans; London, Faber, 1959), pp. 232–41.

THE OLD FARMHOUSE, translated by Waldo Williams. London, Harrap, 1961.

'Pant y Bril' ['Blwyddyn Lwyddiannus'], translated by Glyn Jones: in PLANET, no. 5/6, pp. 69–75 (1971).

BROADCAST DISCUSSIONS

With Saunders Lewis, printed in CREFFT Y STORI FER (Aberystwyth, Y Clwb Llyfrau Cymraeg, 1949), pp. 22–35.

With Aneirin Talfan Davies, printed in D. J. WILLIAMS: CYFROL DEYRNGED (ed. J. Gwyn Griffiths, 1965), pp. 147–59.

A SMALL SELECTION OF WRITINGS ABOUT D. J. WILLIAMS

Gwynfor Evans, Saunders Lewis, 'Two Tributes to D. J. Williams' in THE ANGLO-WELSH REVIEW, vol. 19, pp. 25–31 (1970).

J. Gwyn Griffiths (ed.), D. J. WILLIAMS: CYFROL DEYRNGED. Llandysul, Gwasg Gomer, 1965. This includes studies by Pennar Davies ('HEN WYNEBAU a STORÏAU'R TIR GLAS'), Gwynfor Evans ('Ffydd Wleidyddol'), J. Gwyn Griffiths ('STORÏAU'R TIR COCH a STORÏAU'R TIR DU'), Bobi Jones ('Y Llenor Ymrwymedig'), D. Gwenallt Jones ('Y Fro: Rhydcymerau'), Saunders Lewis ('Arddull'), T. J. Morgan ('Yr Hunangofiannwr'), and Kate Roberts ('Cymdeithas Bro a'r Storïwr').

Dafydd Jenkins, 'D. J. Williams' in GWŶR LLÊN (ed. Aneirin Talfan Davies; London, Griffiths, 1948), pp. 229–40; "Storïau Diweddar D. J. Williams" in Y GENHINEN, vol. vi, pp. 7–12 (1955–6).

Ned Thomas, 'D.J.' in THE WELSH EXTREMIST (London, Gollancz, 1971; paperback edition, Talybont, Y Lolfa, 1973), chapter 7.

Acknowledgements

Quotations appear by permission of D. J. Williams's literary executor; of Gwasg Gomer, Harrap, and Chatto and Windus; of the National Eisteddfod of Wales; and of the Editor of THE ANGLO-WELSH REVIEW. In the quotation of p. 84 Waldo Williams's 'Old Neighbourhood' has been amended to 'Old District' for the sake of consistency with other quotations. Gwenallt's sonnet to Wales is quoted by permission in the translation by Dyfnallt Morgan, published in his study, D. GWENALLT JONES, in this series.

The Author

Dafydd Jenkins is one of several near-namesakes who live in Aberystwyth: among the others are the National Librarian and the author of THE AGRICULTURAL COMMUNITY IN SOUTH-WEST WALES (who is a Senior Tutor in the Extra-mural Department of the University College of Wales). This Dafydd Jenkins is a prolific writer and admits to being a jack-of-all-trades: his first book (TÂN YN LLŶN, 1937) told the story of the Bombing School fire which was a turning-point in D. J. Williams's career; his latest is a text of Welsh medieval law. In the interval he has published biography, travel books, translations from and into Welsh, and literary criticism, including a study of the Welsh novel after Daniel Owen, which was awarded the prose medal of the National Eisteddfod in 1948. He was associated with Aneirin Talfan Davies in founding and editing the monthly HEDDIW (1936–42).

He was born in a London suburb in 1911 (but claims to have been always a Cardiganshire man) and went to Merchant Taylors' School and Sidney Sussex College, Cambridge, where he graduated in natural sciences and law. He has been a practising barrister, secretary for the Welsh Language Petition of 1938–41, farmer, organiser of agricultural co-operation, and teacher of law; he is now Reader in the Department of Law at the University College of Wales, specialising in Legal History and Welsh Law.

This Edition,
designed by Jeff Clements,
is set in Monotype Spectrum 12 Didot on 13 point
and printed on Basingwerk Parchment by
Qualitex Printing Limited, Cardiff

It is limited to 1000 copies of which this is

Copy No.   571